THE GOUGE!

THE GOUGE!

HOW TO BE SMARTER THAN THE SITUATION YOU ARE IN

ADMIRAL BOB HARWARD
US Navy (Ret) SEAL/SWO

Post Hill
PRESS

A POST HILL PRESS BOOK
ISBN: 979-8-88845-868-6
ISBN (eBook): 0979-8-88845-313-1

The Gouge!:
How to Be Smarter Than the Situation You Are In

Cover Art by Marc Salamat
Cover Design by Jim Villaflores

Post Hill Press
New York • Nashville
posthillpress.com

Published in the United States of America
1 2 3 4 5 6 7 8 9 10

To the Girls

TABLE OF CONTENTS

Chapter 1: An Ounce of Gouge Is Worth a Pound of Knowledge 9
Chapter 2: Mission First, People Always.....21
Chapter 3: Purpose Defines You, Embrace It.....31
Chapter 4: Opportunity and the Great Adventure of Life 44
Chapter 5: We Are All Accountable for Ourselves and to Others.....58
Chapter 6: Faith in People Is My Religion.....71
Chapter 7: Never Quit, but Saying No Is Always an Option.....81
Chapter 8: Saying No Is Not Easy.....89
Chapter 9: Your Most Important Bank Account Is Yourself.....97
Chapter 10: Community Matters.....109
Chapter 11: Great Leaders Share Gouge.....118
Chapter 12: Bum Gouge.....128
Chapter 13: Confrontation Can, and Should Be, Productive 133
Chapter 14: Change and Transition Are Inevitable.....144
Chapter 15: As a Human Race, We Are Doing Pretty Damn Good.....149
Chapter 16: Good Gouge.....161

Epilogue.....167
Acknowledgments.....175
About the Author.....176

CHAPTER 1

An Ounce of Gouge Is Worth a Pound of Knowledge

Nothing makes you feel small like the ocean.

Doesn't matter if you're on a warship or in a life raft. The ocean is vast and deep and when you're in the middle of it, it is impossible to feel anything but its power. The ocean can and will swallow you and your ship whole. That's why crews—especially during wartime—band tightly together to survive. On top of the enemy, the sea is always gunning for you.

My father understood that. Standing on the bridge wing of the USS *Sumter* (APA-52), an attack transport ship, on the night of 15 June 1944, Ensign Robert S. Harward felt like the *Sumter* was the only ship in the sea.

It was pitch black and while he knew the other American ships in the task force—all running with no lights—were out there, he couldn't see them. Nor could he see the Japanese ships and submarines stalking them, much less the enemy ashore. A New Yorker from birth, he left the Big Apple for the war in the

Pacific after graduating from the Merchant Marine Academy, Kings Point, in 1943. He was immediately thrust into harm's way. All around him, his shipmates—many still strangers—went about their work. These men, some from the East Coast like my father, while others from the West Coast, and all points in between, were thrown together and ordered to sail into battle.

Combat makes friends of strangers quickly. Especially when you're tasked with launching Marines for the invasion of Saipan, and avoiding intensive fire from enemy artillery, mortars, and kamikazes, much less the rest of the Japanese fleet. It was a life-or-death situation where everyone depended on each other to do their job. The newest or most inexperienced sailors could end up driving or commanding the ship at any time in a battle, a fact many in the US Navy experienced during Pearl Harbor and the rest of the war in the Pacific.

From the start, the crew trained, educated, and proactively shared the best knowledge from the most experienced officers and sailors of all. Everyone knew what everyone else did and could perform the task when it mattered most. They attributed their success to this process and culture and came up with a term for it.

THE GOUGE!

In US Navy jargon, the Gouge is essential information. When my father showed up on the ship, he got the Gouge from his fellow officers and senior enlisted sailors. They told him what he needed to know and care about and what he didn't. Only worry about the important stuff—the stuff that will keep the ship's crew alive and save lives. The Gouge is the heart of the matter. They had a saying: "Live by the Gouge or die by the Gouge." Live by it because it helps you be smarter than any situation you might find yourself in. Without the Gouge, you could die or, even worse, fail your team and the mission.

Since World War II, the meaning of the Gouge has been adopted by many. Naval aviators, who like to take credit for the term, used it to describe the inside scoop. At the United States Naval Academy, the Gouge has its own version. If you ask a midshipman, you're likely to hear the ever-popular story of Big John Griffin and Lester McGill. These two young men roomed together at the Naval Academy and as the story goes, Big John Griffin had been a football star during his four years at the Naval Academy. He tried hard but was only able to maintain a 2.0 grade point average, which just barely kept him in school. Lester, on the other hand, had quite the aptitude for intellectual pursuits. He boasted that during his time in school, he spent a mere two hours in the library yet was able to maintain a 3.8 grade point average. Surprisingly, the two were a good match and supported each other often during their time at school. It was during one of these *supportive* times that the midshipman version of the Gouge emerged.

Big John was dangerously close to failing his thermodynamics class. He knew that he needed a 66 percent to pass the final exam and the class. Anything less would drop his grade point average beyond the 2.0 threshold, and he would fail out of the Naval Academy, which would require him to spend the next five years in the fleet as an enlisted sailor instead of a Naval Officer leading our efforts. The fear of this fate was all the motivation Big John needed to pass this test. Still, as the hours of study accumulated, he was no closer to understanding the course material. The concepts were too complex and the material too vast. He didn't see how he would possibly get a grasp on all this to save his spot at the academy.

As luck would have it, on the day of the exam, Lester was scheduled to take the test during first period. Big John was not scheduled to take the exam until fourth period. And they both had third period free. Now, no one knows exactly what was discussed between these two roommates during their shared free time, but both of them passed that exam. Lester sailed by with a 97 percent and was sure to let everyone know that he barely cracked a book. Big John passed as well, skating by with a 72 percent.

Did they discuss the exam? Was that cheating? What exactly went on in that dorm room? No one knows for sure, but it is assumed that Lester passed along the Gouge to his roommate. If so this ethical dilemma—helping your closest friend for four years who would likely fail and seriously impact the rest of his life—would have been an honor violation. While no one will ever know for sure, Big John went on to an illustrious career as a Marine general, renowned for his combat leadership. This story also serves to reinforce the midshipmen's adage that "an ounce of Gouge is worth a pound of knowledge."

The "real" Gouge is much deeper and more complicated than these simple derivatives. It was created to do more than help people cut corners or find a simple solution. The Gouge is the contract we all have with humanity, sharing the best of everyone for the collective well-being of all. It was always intended to be information you could believe in, people you could trust, and organizations you could rely on because it came from people who wanted the best for you, and therefore good for all. It is building people and our communities. We're on Earth for a short time, never more evident than in combat. We've got to take care and look after each other if we're going to make it. As my father always said, at the end of the day, you will be measured more by what you did for others than what you did for yourself. The Gouge is a testament to this philosophy.

The Gouge functions as an everyday mindset where your ultimate goal is to move yourself and your community, organization, or team forward through the distribution of the best and most relevant information gleaned from hard-learned lessons and experience. Within this philosophy, you create environments for people to benefit from the wisdom of not only your experience but from the collective group, and look for people whose experience you all benefit from. Information gaps are filled almost immediately. Progress emerges organically and persistently from the collective mindset of all.

The Gouge helps you understand how to make decisions that will move you to fulfill your purpose and, at the same time, benefit the team and the organization. In addition to personal advancement, understanding the Gouge is a tremendous leadership tool as it enables you to build and guide successful teams to accomplish any goal or objective by taking care of people and reinforcing their purpose, while meeting common objectives.

Put simply: mission first, people always.

The Gouge philosophy was born in war but is applicable to much more. There are no obstacles when you're following the Gouge, only choices. Each choice is filtered through the collective experience and wisdom of those participating and reinforced by accountability to each other and to yourself, faith in one another, and inherent trust, which facilitates deliberate action. Once a choice is made, you're committed and focused on making it the right choice.

My father applied The Gouge philosophy—experienced-based, and value oriented information—throughout his career and life. He served in the Marshall Islands campaign and the invasions of Saipan and Guam. He transferred to the USS *Fond Du Lac* in September 1944 and trained the crew before taking part in the invasion of Okinawa and the initial landing of American forces at Sasebo, Japan. In 1947, he took part in the evacuation of China as Communist forces took control of the mainland. He went to War in the Pacific in 1943 and came back eight years later in 1951, serving on five different ships. Later, he took part in the embargo of Cuba during the missile crisis as an engineer officer for the carrier USS *Independence*. Finally, he and my family were in Tehran in January 1979 when it fell to Islamic revolutionaries.

He loved the Navy. He loved the camaraderie, the sense of family created by a ship's crew and the shared purpose reinforced by the Gouge. By extension, I was raised on the Gouge. I was introduced to this philosophy at an early age. I have always seen the world through the lens of helping others and easily sharing information, and in every case, I was rewarded for doing so.

Born in Rhode Island in 1956, I grew up in the Navy as my family followed my father's career from Rhode Island to Florida to Hawaii to Virginia and ultimately to Tehran, Iran, where he served as the naval attaché. That is where I grew up from 1968 to 1974, going to an American school, skiing the Elburz Mountains in Northern Iran, and hitchhiking around central Asia and Europe in the summers.

After my senior year in high school, I enlisted in the Navy and went to prep school on my way to the US Naval Academy in Annapolis, Maryland. My dad taught engineering at the US Naval Academy from 1960 through 1962. This is where I believe the Gouge was inculcated at the school and my father with his understanding of the selection process helped make the option of attending available to me. While we never talked about it, I am not sure if it was because he knew how much I would love it or if he was more focused on seeing me gainfully employed and off his books.

Before enrolling at the academy, I attended the Naval Academy Prep School (NAPS) in Newport, Rhode Island, in the summer of 1974. I still remember orientation week when there was tons of new information coming at us: where to go, how to wear a uniform, and who to salute. My head was spinning. On top of this new information, I was also just reacclimating back to the United States after having lived in Iran for the previous seven years. There was a lot to catch up on. I had never been to McDonald's, had a car, or even seen a professional sports game, uncommon for kids my age and unlike all the other students in my class. Even though America was my home, it took some getting used to after such a long stretch away. During orientation, NAPS brought in different seniors from the Naval Academy to get us up to speed. I remember one senior told us: "You guys have heard a lot of stuff today. Some of it is important. Some of it is not. Let me tell you the Gouge. It is the only stuff you need to succeed this year."

He paused to make sure we were all listening.

"Focus on your schoolwork. Make sure you get decent grades and you'll be accepted at the Naval Academy. Nothing else matters. That is the Gouge."

Some of my fellow new recruits might not have even heard this piece of advice. But as soon as I heard "Gouge," my ears perked up. I knew what that term meant and it hit home. It gave me the bottom line: exactly what I needed to focus on to reach my goal. It was precisely what my dad's original intended purpose for the Gouge was and it was what I needed to hear. It served as that beacon that reinforced the philosophy of the midshipmen taking care of each other. That sense of family and community at the school. I knew I could trust and believe in this leader because we shared a purpose, as well as the institution.

After four years at the academy, I wanted to be a SEAL, the ultimate physical warrior who functioned at sea, in the air and on land, but at that point the Navy did not allow it. It was shrinking the SEALs post-Vietnam. The Navy also wanted SEAL candidates who washed out of the training program to have a backup plan. So, first, I tried flight school and served aboard the guided-missile destroyer USS *Scott* (DDG-995) for four years before finally having the opportunity to join the US Navy SEAL family. It was a dream come true and what I had always wanted to do. I felt like I was home and it translated into me being named "Honor Man" of training class 128 in 1984.

More importantly it led to the greatest adventure known to man.

For forty years, I lived a blessed life. I couldn't wait to wake up every day and live every minute. I was part of a community bigger than myself every day with all the best equipment the US government had in its arsenal. I started at SEAL Team THREE, then a tour at Naval Special Warfare Development Group before becoming aide-de-camp to Army General Wayne Downing, Commander of US Special Operations Command (SOCOM), various Special Operations commands, including as General Stan McChrystal's deputy at the Joint Special

Operations Command (JSOC) and worked for General Dave Petraeus for two years in Afghanistan. I served as Marine General Jim Mattis' deputy four times and worked in the White House for Condoleezza Rice, Steve Hadley, and Fran Townsend during the Bush administration.

I circumnavigated and visited every country on the South American continent and saw duty in Japan, the Philippines, Bosnia, Kuwait, Afghanistan, Yemen, Iraq, and many more. I ran security for the 2000 Olympics in Australia and led Special Operations Forces from ten countries in combat from the US, Canada, Germany, New Zealand, Australia, Poland, Denmark, United Kingdom, Turkey, and Kuwait—in invasions of Afghanistan and Iraq. I hunted down our most vicious enemies around the world, led rule of law, prisons, and detention operations in Afghanistan for two years, and commanded thousands of troops throughout the Middle East in both peace and war.

After retiring from the Navy in November 2013, I had the privilege and pleasure of serving as the chief executive for the largest defense company in the world, running their business in the United Arab Emirates and the Middle East, negotiating and delivering billions of dollars in business. I saw this as getting a doctorate in international business, while enjoying another great adventure.

Along the way, I broke a world record by parachute jumping onto Mount Everest and was asked by President Donald Trump to serve as his National Security Advisor before turning it down. All these amazing adventures—and many more—were informed and guided by the Gouge.

I believe that the Gouge Philosophy is more important now than it ever has been.

The Gouge originated at a time when information was hard to come by. Families and communities were key sources of essential and trusted information that you could depend on, as other sources were limited, especially in the military, where you were isolated from many aspects of society.

The crews of ships and their families had to depend on—and trust—experience-based information from each other to make important decisions. In today's world, we are inundated by a constant and overwhelming wave of data, gossip, and news trying to influence us, tell us what *facts* are, and in most cases, try to sell us a product or convince us of an agenda. There is no doubt that the internet and social media provide all the information you need and want, including a lot of good Gouge, but it is also used to push agendas. Your best interests may not be part of that agenda. The long-term impact of the internet on communities and society is still not clear. Yet many develop a trust and believe in these platforms and systems to make key decisions. Many do not understand that this many not be good Gouge for them depending on their situation. The internet can affirm any bias or point of view, which can be harmful unless you have a way to filter it. That is where the Gouge comes in because it provides a value structure—a North Star if you will—to filter the deluge of information available in our society.

Don't forget the Gouge was adopted by warfighters during World War II who needed the best information in a timely manner to survive when information was hard to come by. My father always reinforced that most people like to talk, but the most valuable skill set is being able to listen and assimilate information. That's why the Gouge is important. It gets people to focus, listen, and digest the irrefutable, and applicable information that you can trust and rely on, as well as the people sharing it with you.

The more experience you have with the Gouge, the better you become at identifying good from bad Gouge. You quickly learn to sift through and sort out the information that is not necessary or helpful. You eventually learn to study and understand the source of your Gouge, the context in which you are receiving it and the timing. You learn who you can trust and believe in. All these things are vital to getting the most out of the information, but more importantly your commitment to share good Gouge, and help other people as they help you. In essence, you have a robust and effective filtering system for the information coming at you. The Gouge is the philosophy and culture that affirms how you think, not what you think.

The end of my father's journey as a US Naval Officer and the beginning of my adventure of a lifetime. He knew I would love the US Navy as much as he did. My father's last words to the Naval Officer Recruiter presiding over my enlistment and his retirement as he pointed at me, "He's all yours, send me a postcard and let me know how it works out for you."

At the end of the day, the Gouge reinforces a belief in people and the power of collective action and sticking together and making sure we're all moving toward a common goal that is good for everyone. I look back on all the folks who have worked for me and I think I made a difference for them, but more importantly, each and every one had a powerful impact on me. This great adventure of life that I've been on was enabled by all those I met, served with, and loved because we lived by the Gouge and fulfilled our contract with one another in taking care of each other.

CHAPTER 2

Mission First, People Always

Immediately after the attacks on September 11, 2001, that killed more than 3,000 Americans, we left for the invasion of Afghanistan, and by October 1, 2001, we had SEALs on the ground hunting down those who had attacked us.

My job was to lead several hundred of our best US Special Operations warriors, as well as our coalition Special Operations partners, into combat. A few of us had combat experience from the Gulf War, Bosnia, Panama, and Somalia. But for the vast majority, this was their first test. As we prepared, their emotions were swirling. Fear. Doubt. Even excitement. It's a weird cocktail when you're about to go into harm's way. There was no place we wanted to be more than carrying out this mission, but we also understood our country might be asking for the last full measure. The thought of losing more Americans, and more importantly, my guys, was front of mind.

Before we put one boot on Afghan soil, I pulled the force together. I wanted them to know exactly what the priorities were so they could act accordingly.

It was simple and summarized in three priorities:

1. We would conduct every mission we were assigned.

Our nation recruited us, trained us, and spent a hell of a lot of resources to ensure we were the best trained, best equipped, and best-prepared force in the world and now we were needed. It was now time to pay the dividends on that investment the American people had made in us.

2. We would do the right thing, as we would live with the ramifications for the rest of our lives.

We were fighting a group of poor, unsophisticated, and ill-equipped tribesmen. We could go anywhere in Afghanistan we wanted at the time of our choosing, and we had all the tools in the American arsenal to support us. I warned them the biggest challenge was separating the armed combatants from the civilians. Just because many Afghans had weapons, it did not make them the enemy. Most people in Afghanistan just wanted to live in peace, while struggling to survive.

By the time of our invasion in 2001, SEALs and Special Operations Forces had years of experience with night vision, and hence our operations in Afghanistan were predominantly night-oriented to minimize risk and ensure our warfighting advantage. With this advantage we could clearly see the enemy to target them, while they would be hard-pressed to do the same. We had the drop on them and could neutralize a threat if necessary because our laser designators confirmed that our first shot would be fatal if necessary. I stressed how we needed to do the right thing, by doing no harm to those who are not combatants.

This is how we would win this war of ideology with the people of Afghanistan.

The last point was most important to me.

3. Nothing we did was worth losing one person from our team.

If we went on a mission and things went wrong, I told them to pull back and regroup. There was no reason to be dangerously aggressive as the odds were stacked in our favor. If we couldn't do a mission based on a deteriorating situation or changing dynamics, we could do it again later any night we choose. The enemy wasn't going anywhere. I knew we could get them at any time we wanted, so the most important thing to me was making sure I took everyone home when we were done.

We paraphrased it into a mantra: Mission first, people always.

By March 2002, we had eviscerated all those responsible for the attacks of September 11, 2001, by either capturing or killing them and causing the rest to flee the country to other safe havens, where we would get them some time in the future. And we did it all without losing a single man. It all came down to our mantra.

Mission first, people always.

This is the core principle of the Gouge. How we prioritize it and contribute to it determines our fate as human beings. It is applicable in combat, business, any team effort and just life in general. We all have the opportunity every day to make ourselves and others better every day. Any team you're on—especially if you're a leader—you are a participant in human development. If we can take care of people and each other, the rest of it will come. The best organizations balance the mission and the people.

This is really the reason why the Gouge is so important, because at each level and each opportunity people must come first and our mission always but it doesn't work well if you don't have people looking after each other to build trust and confidence: the purpose of their life.

That is what the Gouge reinforces.

I believe if your approach and understanding is to take care of people, they'll take care of the business. They'll make those sacrifices that you see in the military. That reinforced purpose and the belief of why these guys will sacrifice and do that additional work and take those additional challenges because they want to be part of that successful team at the same time, knowing that the team is going to take care of them, and that's the Gouge.

It's like that story from the Naval Academy Preparatory School. That guy told us all we had to remember was to take care of our grades. Get your grades and you'll get it. I thought *Hell yes. That's a guy I believe in. He's told me what I need to know. I have trust in him and I have trust in the institution if the leaders are treating us that way.*

The foundation of the Gouge is all about building that trust and confidence. You build that trust and confidence in each other by making sure the people involved have a voice in the organization and the mission. The messy part of people is that they're unpredictable. They can be selfish, so part of the Gouge is instilling that contract with humanity: knowing that I'm going to do my best for you because you're going to do your best for me and when that happens, we're all going to be in good shape.

I was the executive officer of a forward deployed SEAL unit, the number two guy working for the commanding officer, running the platoons and SEALs. We were stationed in the Philippines and trained with our counterparts in Australia, Indonesia, and Malaysia. That unit is now based in Guam.

It was early June 1991 when meteorologists were predicting Mount Pinatubo was going to erupt. US forces evacuated Clark Air Force Base personnel and families to the naval base at Subic Bay. Lo and behold, Mount Pinatubo erupted on 12 June. The volcanic ash spewed up a couple hundred miles into the Iona sphere, where wind currents moved it at altitude.

While we knew it had erupted the effects had not been adequately assessed for our location. It was a Saturday morning and my family and I lived on base. We were about two miles from where our unit was located so my normal Saturday drill was to wake up, run down to our unit, read the message traffic of what's going on in the region, and then come home for lunch.

I ran down. It was a nice sunny day. I was in my office working, and all of a sudden, it was pitch black outside. I couldn't see anything. I went outside of the building and could not see my hand in front of my face. It was that pitch black and it was raining ash. It took only a few minutes before it covered my shoes. It was about a quarter-inch deep. I went back into the office and started making calls to my SEAL platoons, checking to make sure everyone was okay. A half hour later, the building started shaking. I ran out just as it collapsed. It was clear that the infrastructure wasn't built to withstand the weight of the ash. They don't get snow in the Philippines. I ran into another one of our buildings and started making calls when I felt the building shake. I ran out just before it collapsed. There was one remaining building—our garage.

The building could house eight vehicles. The only reason it hadn't collapsed was because the roofs were reinforced with beams because we had installed lifts to be able to pull engines out of our vehicles or load ammunition and equipment pallets onto trailers.

The ash was getting deep. I got a SEAL on duty to run over to the barracks, which is probably a mile, and told everyone to report to the headquarters. Everyone who was there grabbed shovels and brooms and headed to the command.

The green, lush countryside was covered in a blanket of three to four feet of ash, which had the same composition as wet cement. No colors other than black and gray. The trees looked burned. It is what I imagined a nuclear holocaust would look like.

The overall situation was catastrophic as buildings on the base and the adjoining town were collapsing and trapping and killing people. Several Americans evacuated from Clark perished when the gym they were housed in collapsed. We couldn't clear the ash fast enough.

Once all the ash was cleared off our boats at the command—to ensure they did not sink—we shifted our attention to our families. The ash was so deep we could no longer drive on the roads. Walking was the only option, but it was like wading through knee-deep snow. It took considerable effort to hike a few dozen yards. One of the SEALs got a bulldozer—how, I will never know—and carved a path from the command to the living quarters. We cleared roofs and prepared families for evacuation as we knew this was an unsustainable situation and it would be months before life would return to normal.

Our next priority was food and water. It became clear this was not something we were going to recover from anytime soon.

The Navy recalled the entire fleet in the Pacific to start evacuating people. We had probably one hundred families between ours at the unit and the families that had come from Clark Air Force Base. In a matter of a few days, we were able to evacuate all of them to Guam, where they got flights back to the US.

We got the families out and were using these bulldozers to clear the ash and debris in order to recover all of our essential weapons and communication equipment. For the next two days, we found our weapons and crypto for our radios. We salvaged engines and started to rebuild the storage structures. We salvaged the barracks and set up shop in the garage. After seventy-two hours of non-stop, around-the-clock work, we were able to give the team a break to let them sleep and recover. I was in our makeshift headquarters when one of my guys walked in. I could tell from his face he didn't have good news.

"Hey, sir, we got a problem," he said.

"What do you mean 'we got a problem'?"

"I forgot about a safe."

We'd spent the last days recovering everything and doing an inventory to ensure we had all our essential and critical equipment. A uniquely difficult task that we had never anticipated, planned, or trained for.

"What do you mean you 'forgot about a safe'?"

"Well, we had this one safe with all the crypto in it and I forgot about it."

Crypto is life or death. Without it, we couldn't communicate securely. From the start of our careers, our instructors beat into us that you can't lose it and your career depends on accountability for it.

"OK, you have the privilege of going back and telling all the guys to get up, get them back here to the command; we're going back to that field everything was dumped in to find the safe."

The SEAL did an about-face and rallied the guys. No one complained. We all banded together and headed down to a football-sized field where the base was dumping all the ash and debris. The pile was about twenty feet high and stretched about one hundred yards long and fifty yards wide. We split up into teams and started to comb the field. It was back-breaking work and soon everyone was covered in ash and soot. We searched for two days until we finally uncovered the safe. We scooped it up and took it back to the garage, where we opened it and verified all of the crypto was intact. Everything was still secure.

He thought this was the worst thing he'd ever done in his life. To be fair to him, he had screwed up in an absolutely ridiculous scenario. It's not like we are trained to handle the aftermath of a volcanic eruption. But the team shrugged. We'll go get it. They were gracious and treated him like a hero for coming forth with the problem. They embraced the Gouge philosophy because it could've easily been one of them.

This was our family. We had the same purpose and goals. We took care of each other first and the mission was completed with that understanding.

The Gouge is based on human-to-human connection through action, information, and trust. Living the Gouge means serving your purpose so that the team excels. It also means taking care of your fellow person, as you would have them do for you. Success comes from the people, nothing else.

I have been retired from the military for nearly a decade, and yet I have never been more concerned for our military and what is happening in the ranks due to the ungodly rate of suicides. We have never invested more resources into the training and education of our military forces in our history, and we have the most professional, well-prepared, and capable fighting force in the world. But there's a huge lingering problem.

A testament to this is the low casualty rate over twenty years of constant conflict in Afghanistan, Iraq, Syria, Yemen, and other locations. We have lost more than 7,000 service members overseas since September 11, 2001. While each is tragic, it is almost a miracle that the numbers are so low, as at no time in our history of warfare, much less over a twenty-year period, have we had such a low rate of casualties. I mourn each and every life and will always have the families who live with that loss in my heart and thoughts.

But if those numbers are shockingly low, the deaths in our other war are shockingly high. During the same time—2001 to 2021—we have had an unprecedented epidemic of suicides, losing over 38,000 of our military members and other veterans to this tragic and avoidable fate. Regardless of your prioritization—mission first, people always, or vice versa—it is clear we are losing the war for our people. There is no doubt that we have the best trained and most professional military force in our history. But we need to be cognizant of the fact that the personal lives of military members are just as important as their professional lives, and that well could be the more important battle we are fighting.

We must never forget we're in the human development business.

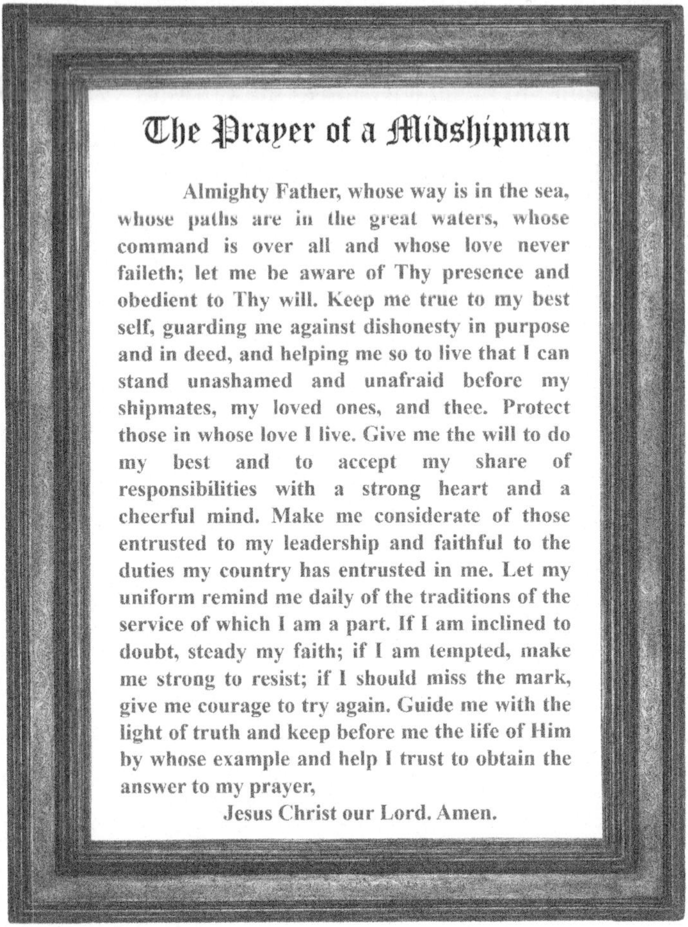

The Prayer of a Midshipman

Almighty Father, whose way is in the sea, whose paths are in the great waters, whose command is over all and whose love never faileth; let me be aware of Thy presence and obedient to Thy will. Keep me true to my best self, guarding me against dishonesty in purpose and in deed, and helping me so to live that I can stand unashamed and unafraid before my shipmates, my loved ones, and thee. Protect those in whose love I live. Give me the will to do my best and to accept my share of responsibilities with a strong heart and a cheerful mind. Make me considerate of those entrusted to my leadership and faithful to the duties my country has entrusted in me. Let my uniform remind me daily of the traditions of the service of which I am a part. If I am inclined to doubt, steady my faith; if I am tempted, make me strong to resist; if I should miss the mark, give me courage to try again. Guide me with the light of truth and keep before me the life of Him by whose example and help I trust to obtain the answer to my prayer,

Jesus Christ our Lord. Amen.

The framed Midshipman's Prayer that my father gave me and I always kept on my desk. It is an affirmation of our contract with humanity and our fellow shipmates.

CHAPTER 3

Purpose Defines You, Embrace It

I'm going to get these guys killed.

The words rattled in my brain. I was nauseous to my core. My confidence shattered; I raced to the head and threw up. It made me physically ill thinking that I was sending these men to an early grave.

It was March 2003 and we were hours away from launching an invasion of Iraq. I'd already led Joint (US Navy SEALs, Army Special Forces, and Air Force Special Operations Forces) and Combined (Canadian, German, New Zealand, Australian, Norwegian, Dane, and Turkish) forces into Afghanistan in October 2001, immediately after the attacks of September 11, 2001, in New York, Washington, and Pennsylvania. I returned home without losing a man. After spending a few months with the family in San Diego, I deployed to Kuwait to plan and prepare for the possible invasion of Iraq. We didn't think it was possible as no one seemed to support it, and invading Iraq, with a large structured military force, was a much different problem, but our job was to position and plan in case we got the call.

Now, hours from launch, I'd just been told my men weren't confident in the plan we'd been practicing for months. I returned to my desk and started to review the mission again—from the top—but as I flipped to each briefing slide, the words in my head got heavier. Were we planning a mission that was going to get a bunch of young men whom I loved killed?

My job was to lead some of America's most elite operators into Iraq. Based at a Kuwait naval base, my multinational task force had a thousand men ranging from SEALs to Naval Special Warfare boat crews, SEAL delivery vehicles and Air Force Special Operations helicopters and crews, to Explosive Ordnance Disposal (EOD) teams and even Navy fleet assets. Special Operations units from Kuwait and Poland were also part of our team. I spent my days in a primitive command center doing back-to-back-to-back video conferences with commanders in Washington, Qatar, Florida, and California as we hashed out what an invasion of Iraq might look like.

The initial plan was for Special Operations Forces to go in before the land invasion. But as we started our assessment of the waterways, we analyzed the first Gulf War where Saddam Hussein ordered the destruction of crude oil facilities to wreak havoc on our forces and the ecology and suggested that the US was responsible for this. He had ordered all the oil wellheads in Kuwait blown off, leaving the country a nightmare, and we had to plan for Iraq doing it again.

Ninety percent of Iraq's oil was exported through two gas and oil platforms (GOPLATs). Oil was pumped from Platform

1—Mina Al Bakr—to Platform 2—Khawr Al Amaya. The pipes from the land-based pumping stations reached approximately ten miles out to the first platform. Between the two platforms lay twelve miles of pipeline—two pipes, each six feet in diameter. The platforms were like large gas station where supertankers pulled up and filled their tanks. Mina Al Bakr alone was capable of filling four tankers the size of the Exxon Valdez at one time.

Our intelligence determined Saddam could blow up the oil pumping stations at the start of the war, creating a huge environmental disaster that would pale in comparison to the first Gulf War because this one would flood the Arabian Gulf with hundreds of thousands of gallons of oil.

The platforms became target number one.

"Hey, we need to seize these at the very start of this to ensure they do not damage them or blow them," I said to my superiors at Special Operations Command in Tampa. "Plus, this would maintain a lifeline for the follow-on government, much less anyone else to help build Iraq." Oil was the biggest commodity and the chief source of revenue in the country's post-Saddam reconstruction. But the commanders—senior generals from the Air Force, Army, and Marines—planning the invasion felt they needed to go first, crossing the border with their land forces and air support to maintain the element of surprise. This debate went on for months.

My immediate boss was Major General Gary Harrell, Central Command (CENTCOM) Commander responsible for the Special Operations Forces in the Middle East. He was based in Qatar with the rest of the staff planning the invasion. He hated the idea of hitting the oil platforms first. Harrell didn't see the value in the mission. I sent Captain Brian Losey to Qatar to sell the mission and get it approved. Being an operator and SEAL commander, I figured Losey could get them to understand the strategic ramifications. More importantly, he was a no-nonsense, hard—both physically and mentally—SEAL who I knew would accomplish the mission of reinforcing the purpose of the operation. Even though the planners and generals didn't believe in it, the fact that we highlighted it, made them accountable and responsible for it, in case the Iraqis blew up the platform, and we didn't have a plan to stop it. They had to support it, but I knew it would take them a while to come to terms with the fact.

Losey went to work on Harrell with my guidance, but we never really knew where we stood. We never got confirmation, even as more and more of the planners saw the value in it, until March 21. General Tommy Franks, commander of Central Command, called all the commanders together and told us we were going to invade Iraq in forty-eight hours.

"Harward, you guys take down the oil platforms during the night, and everyone else goes immediately after that," Franks told the assembled commanders.

I was in shock. I was going to lead the invasion of a second country. It started in Afghanistan in 2001. Now I got to lead the invasion of Iraq. It was a culmination of my purpose in life and justification for all those years of being a SEAL. This was a dream come true, but on the flipside, I didn't think it was a good move. We didn't need to invade Iraq, nor did we have the support of the world. I didn't think it would end well over the long haul, but it wasn't my call. I passed those concerns on to my shipmate at the White House, Bill McRaven, who would go on to lead the

Osama bin Laden raid years later. I thought there was a better strategy for Iraq, but no one asked me.

After the video conference with Franks, I gathered my staff. "Get everybody together in three hours. I want everyone here," I said.

When everyone was mustered, I walked to the front.

"Guys, we're going in forty-eight hours," I said.

The energy changed in the room. The tension of waiting was replaced with the anticipation of action. No more rehearsals. No more meetings. No more crafting checklists. We were about to test our plan and this time the enemy was going to have a vote.

"Go do your final checks; go do what you got to do, but the world will be watching what you're going to do here shortly," I said. "They won't know who you are, but they'll know what you accomplished. Any questions?"

No one said a word, and everyone went off to get ready. I headed back to my room where I started to review the execution checklist. There were three different groups—one for each oil platform and one attacking the pumping station on the peninsula. All three targets had to be done simultaneously. We were fixated on preventing an environmental disaster.

We had hundreds of people, helicopters, mini-subs, and boats doing three simultaneous targets separated by great distances, so it was complex. One of the largest missions in the history of Special Operations. I was surprised by how confident in the plan I was. Each component had rehearsed their parts. We had practiced on off-set locations. We flew the routes in a simulated fashion. We had done probably thirty to forty rehearsals. My only concern was the outcome and if I would get some of our SEALs killed.

The platforms were perfect SEAL missions. We could come from under the water and they'll never see us. But the Al-Faw peninsula had mud banks that stretched for hundreds of yards out from the shore and the high-water line. You physically couldn't come from the sea, which is what SEALs do best. You could not transverse the mud by swimming or crawling over it. You had to walk through it at the pace of one hundred yards every ten or fifteen minutes because it was so thick and deep. There was no way to sneak up on the pumping station and you'd become an easy target if seen. We had to fly to the X, meaning the helicopters would drop the assault team on the target in a frontal air assault.

About four hours after the announcement, I got a knock at my door. Outside was SEAL Commander Adam. He was leading the assault on the Al-Faw peninsula.

"Boss, I need to talk to you," he said.

"Sure; come on in," I responded. I waved Adam into the room and motioned to a chair nearby.

I closed the door and sat down across from him. His usual straight back was stooped like a Sherpa hauling a load up Mount Everest. Bags hung under his eyes and his usual confidence was replaced with nervous energy. Whatever he needed to say wasn't easy. After I sat down, he looked me in the eye.

"Boss, me and the boys believe they're going to shoot us out of the sky and we're going to be slaughtered on this assault."

My worst fear.

For the next few minutes, we talked through the mission and intelligence assessment. It was a high-risk mission, especially if the Iraqis had RPGs. We saw what a well-placed shot could do in Somalia and Afghanistan. But, based on intelligence assessments,

I was confident the Iraqis didn't have that kind of firepower. The country was preparing for an invasion and these were isolated platforms and almost impossible to defend. There was no reason to waste RPGs there. They might get some shots off with their rifles, but the assault team would be on top of them before they could mount a defense.

"Like I told you, they're going to be isolated," I said. "They won't fight."

But I didn't have to go on the mission. Adam did, and by the look on his face he had his doubts.

"Look, Adam, if you really believe this, you disagree with my assessment, I'll go back to Franks and tell him we can't do this mission," I said. "We can't do it. The risk has grown. It's unsupportable."

Granted, we were going to look a little dumb because we'd been pushing this and rehearsing it for four months. But if Adam really believed that we were going to get people killed, I was willing to do that. He had the mission. I delegated that authority and responsibility to him to determine if it was achievable.

"You go back to the boys and have this discussion," I told Adam. "I don't want to have it with them. You're the commander; you're the guy doing the raid. You have this discussion with them, and you come back to me. And I will go with whatever you want to do on this thing."

Adam nodded his head in agreement and left. But I couldn't shake the conversation. It left me unsettled. I couldn't focus on the mission briefing. The conversation nagged at me. I was asking a guy to willingly risk his life when I knew he had previously almost lost his life in a bizarre situation that precipitated the US invasion of Panama in December 1989.

He was detained and subsequently tortured in 1989 which precipitated the US invasion of Panama.

Adam and his wife were stationed at one of our SEAL forward-based locations in Panama. He had been out to dinner and was coming back to the base near Panama City. Unbeknownst to him, a car filled with four young officers had arrived at the checkpoint about five minutes before them. When the young officers pulled up, the comandancia soldiers tried to arrest them so they ran the checkpoint. The comandancia opened fire and shot at them, hitting two. One died and another was wounded.

Minutes later and with no knowledge of what had just transpired, Adam and his wife pulled up to the same checkpoint. He was dragged from his car and taken to a prison where he was assaulted and tortured throughout the night. When he was released the next day, President George H. W. Bush ordered the invasion of Panama, which I also helped plan. Adam was hospitalized for several weeks based on how badly they had beaten and tortured him.

A knock at the door a couple of hours later broke the tension. It was Adam with his decision. He still looked beaten up, but he held his head high this time.

"Boss, we still think there's a high probability we're all going to be killed," he said, pausing slightly before delivering the verdict.

"But we will do the mission."

"Okay, Adam," I said.

There wasn't much else to say. I closed the door, threw up, and collapsed in my chair, exhausted. I sat for a few minutes at my desk. Fourteen years after nearly losing his life, instigating an invasion halfway across the world launched by President George

W. Bush, Adam was willing to risk his life in an operation that he did not believe would succeed.

For Adam and the boys, it came down to purpose, a key tenet of the Gouge. Leaders and organizations reinforce and leverage purpose. You see it in the military, you see it in business, you see it in teams. It's somewhat undeniable. If Gouge is about the information that links all of us together, our purpose is the bedrock on which Gouge is built. It determines who you are, reinforces your belief, and ultimately determines your success.

In the military, we reinforce that purpose of doing what our nation needs to do to remain a country whose purpose is life, liberty, and the pursuit of happiness. This is what makes us a great nation, in that we are willing to use our most precious assets—our people, like Adam and his team—to fight for those same principles anywhere in the world.

Adam was a US Naval Academy graduate and a Naval Officer. He was willing to risk his life for a greater purpose. The Gouge was part of the contract between me and Adam so that we knew we were part of the same family. He knew I'd listen to him. I knew he had concerns but not because he doubted me or our purpose. His concerns were technical—if you can refer to life-or-death choices as something that clinical—but we both understood our purpose. We shared a macro purpose of serving our men and the mission. Our micro missions were married toward the same goal. Mine was to complete three missions and contribute to a much bigger battle plan. His was to take the pumping station on the Al Faw peninsula.

But we both shared the burden of taking care of the men—the ones who carry the day. Adam knew it. I knew it. That's why

I sent him back to talk to them one more time. This time armed with more Gouge than before. Deep down I know our shared purpose would win the day, but I also would have gone back to Franks if that is what Adam wanted.

Your purpose defines you. It also drives your beliefs in yourself and how others believe in you. The Gouge reinforces and codifies that purpose—that belief in yourself and your organization. Good leaders reinforce and leverage that purpose to achieve those goals, but it all starts with you and your acceptance of your purpose, whether you were able to, as those who serve.

That's the Gouge.

Understand that purpose is fickle. Sometimes you find it, and other times, it finds you. Adam and I, as well as those that served, were able to choose our paths. We loved and cherished every moment of it, understanding the great sacrifice, risk, and hardship that came with it. Often, however, purpose finds you. You're forced to accept it. I have lived around the world and seen the masses toil at hard labor and in extreme conditions just to be able to send a few dollars home to their families, who are thereby able to survive on this income. There are numerous countries where the largest portion of their GDP (the country's gross domestic product) comes from this remittance from those working outside the country. All these laborers I encounter are dedicated to this purpose, and even though few choose it, most embrace it.

It's the only way to be successful. That is really the first test of your purpose. Can you embrace it? If you can't, that's not your purpose. Adam went back to his men and told them what I'd said. They knew my intent. They understood why I was comfortable with the mission despite the risk of flying to the X. Adam could go back and share good Gouge with them so they—collectively—could decide to go or not go.

They decided to go.

That didn't give me a lot of relief.

In my mind, I assumed responsibility for the mission and the fear that is always there when you're leading men in harm's way started to grow bigger and heavier. My mind wouldn't let go of Adam's words until it turned them into a mantra that settled into a steady beat in my head. For the next forty-eight hours, as we prepared to launch, I couldn't eat. I spent the few hours I had to sleep staring at the ceiling. I was a wreck, but there was no alternative.

When we failed to kill Saddam with a precision bomb and cruise missile strike on March 20, reports began to come in from the Iraqi southern oilfields that six wellheads had been destroyed and were burning. There also were reports of the evacuation of Pakistani and Indian workers from the GOPLATs. Our intelligence spotted "thugs with large boxes" arriving on the platforms. Fearing that these were the first moves in Saddam's "scorched earth" plan, CENTCOM moved up the start of the ground invasion and gave us the green light to launch.

Before launch, I went and saw every guy going on the mission. I looked them in the eye. I gave them my guidance before going to the operations center to oversee all three raids. My greatest concern was the helicopter with Adam and his men were flying on into Al-Faw. I wasn't worried about the oil platforms. Those teams were SEALs in the water, in their environment.

I felt the most incredible adrenaline buzz when the first groups launched, and the radio chatter crackled over the speakers in the command center. But in the back of my mind, I was praying every second. The twin assaults on the GOPLATs started at 10:25 p.m. The assault teams achieved total surprise and Platform 1 was taken by the SEALs in minutes. Platform 2 fell to the Polish GROM next. A total of thirty-two prisoners were taken. No fatalities on either side. Success in my book.

With the platforms secure, EOD teams searched for explosives. The thugs' boxes had explosives and dive gear to place charges on the submerged structure. We'd successfully averted our worst fears about ecological and infrastructure damage.

As we attacked the platforms, Adam and his men closed on the Mina Al Bakr oil terminal on the Al-Faw peninsula. Resistance was light and no one had RPGs, to my relief. The SEALs came under sporadic fire from an Iraqi bunker until two thousand-pound and one five-hundred-pound bombs released from an F-18, as well as 40mm and 105mm shells from an AC-130, destroyed the bunker. The terminal fell after that, with no SEALs killed or wounded. For the next twenty-four hours, the SEALs and EOD cleared the platform of explosives and waited to hand it over to the Marines.

A day later, Adam and his men returned to Kuwait eager for another mission, their purpose validated and renewed by the success of the mission.

Unlike the invasion of Afghanistan, our Maritime SOF (Special Operations Force) capabilities were critical in securing the oil infrastructure and clearing all the waterways of mines at the start of invading Iraq.

Clearing ships in Iraqi waterways. Each and every mission was completely different, requiring our team's ships to adapt and overcome incessantly.

CHAPTER 4

Opportunity and the Great Adventure of Life

When I was a sophomore in high school, my father suggested I hitchhike from Tehran—where we lived—to India.

It all started over a drink. My father was having a cocktail after work and asked me what I planned to do for the summer. He was a product of the 1950s, which meant happy hour started at five. With a Johnny Walker in hand, my dad threw out the idea.

"Why don't you go somewhere?" my father said as he sipped his drink. "Go see the world."

My father was a global type of guy. He'd been all over the world in the Navy, fought in the Pacific, then sailed in the Atlantic, the Mediterranean, and the Indian Ocean. He was a traveler and thought the world was a good place. He embraced people and instilled that in us as children. He encouraged us to get out of the house and go places. My family traveled throughout Iran itself, skiing in the mountains, and going up to the Caspian Sea, the Dasht-e Kavir Desert, and the Arabian Gulf.

The sixties were a much different era than today. The West was embraced throughout the Middle East. We were the most favored partner of Iran, Afghanistan, Pakistan, and the region at large. In terms of crime, in terms of public safety, it was never an issue, which was why my father was pitching a trek across Iran, through Afghanistan and Pakistan to India.

At the time, pilgrims from America and Europe were going there for spiritual guidance and to smoke dope, but also for transcendental meditation, to become one with themselves. The Beatles were the highest-profile pilgrims, but a lot of Americans were headed down the Hippie Trail that cut through Afghanistan and Pakistan on the way to enlightenment. I just wanted the great adventure.

"OK, how do I do that?" I asked.

My father took a sip of his drink and moved from the bar area to his favorite chair.

"I don't know," he said. "Go find a friend."

He reached into his pocket and pulled out his bankroll.

"Here are a couple of bucks; just make sure you're back by the time school starts."

I think he may have just wanted to get rid of me for the summer, but deep down I knew he had another reason. It was all about the Gouge. When opportunity—especially high adventure presents itself—take it.

"Listen, your life is going to be mapped by people you come in contact with and you're involved with; make the most of it, go do it," he said.

I listened. I loved my dad and I always thought he had my best interests in mind, so when he said it, it just sounded like a good idea to me.

I took the money and retreated to my room to plan. The next morning, I knew what I was going to do that summer.

"OK, Dad, I'm going to head east through Afghanistan, Pakistan, India and see how far I can get," I said.

My father nodded in agreement as I laid out the details. Bus routes to Mashed in northeast Iran, and then hitch to the Afghan border and cross into the town or Herat. From there, stops in Kandahar, Kabul, and Peshawar. When I was done, he had a smile on his face.

"That's a great idea," he said, eating breakfast before heading to the American embassy. "But you got to have someone to go with you. Two is one. One is none, so always have a buddy with you, someone you can rely on and depend on. That way if you're in trouble, you need something, someone can look after you."

That day at school I hit up my friends between classes. At first, they thought I was crazy. It wasn't hitchhiking. That was common practice. As a fifteen-year-old kid, that's just what we did to get around. Everyone in the region hitchhiked. No one would do you harm. It wasn't even conceivable. Hitchhiking was accepted practice and being an American was helpful because everyone wanted to pick you up to practice their English. If you spoke Farsi, like I did, it was mind-blowing. All my friends came to embrace the idea.

The hurdle was spending the summer on the road, Jack Kerouac–style, without parents. It was one thing to hang around Tehran. It was another to travel across central Asia to the Indian subcontinent. But by the end of the day, I had four friends onboard. Now we had to convince their parents, who were in Iran working on oil and gas projects. My father spent the next few weeks going with me to talk with their families about the trip and help convince the parents it was a great opportunity. Our barnstorming tour secured five friends, making our party six—each of us had a swim buddy.

Swim buddy is a SEAL term for someone you depend on, believe in and can trust your life too. In the Navy they use the term *shipmate*. Your swim buddy looks out for you and you for them. They are also the person to call you out and give you advice. And when you're conducting missions or hazardous training, they are there to provide an additional safety perspective to keep you alive.

In the first phase of SEAL training Basic Underwater Demolition School (BUD/S), you're not allowed to be at more than arm's length from your swim buddy. It's a safety mechanism, as there are hundreds of you in the freezing ocean at night and all experience the effects of hypothermia (a life-threatening lowering of the core body temperature). You really trust your life to your swim buddy in case either of you reaches the point of succumbing to that fate and passing out. At that point your swim buddy is there to get you to safety or signal instructors to act.

I was blessed with the best swim buddies, starting with my trip to Afghanistan, all the way up to my SEAL training. But Rick Velchek is the hall-of-famer. We have a famous swim during BUD/S where we do two miles in the freezing Pacific Ocean to earn our wetsuit. I went hypothermic during the swim. I finished it, but I don't remember it because I passed out. Rick got me to the finish and out of the water. When we got to Hell Week, I was concerned that I would not be able to survive the effects of hypothermia, reinforced by a week of no sleep. I knew that

Hell Week always resulted in an 80 to 90 percent attrition rate. It is considered to be the biggest determinant in who makes it through training. I was concerned that I would fall victim to the conditions where my mind could not override it.

A quick primer on Hell Week: It is held on the third week of the First Phase and is five and a half days of being cold, wet, and tired. You don't get more than four hours of sleep during the entire week and candidates remain in constant motion: sit-ups to push-ups to rolling in the surf. Instructors force the boat teams to paddle their boats, carry them across the sand, and do log PT—lifting a heavy log with your teammates. This is an endless cycle performed to exhaustion. Teammates pull passed-out buddies out of the water during swims and paddles or out of their food during meals. The training is as hard on your body as it is on your mind. But at the end of the day, instructors aren't counting reps or checking times. They are testing one thing—desire.

Do you want to be a SEAL?

Hell Week will get the answer and if you make it, one thing is certain: you'll never quit.

As we were resting in a tent a few hours before the start of Hell Week, I smelled a strong odor of alcohol. I asked Rick if he had been drinking and it was clear to me he was seriously inebriated. He'd spent the Sunday afternoon before we reported to the tent drinking and partying at a Chargers football game.

"Are you insane?" I said. "We're going to start Hell Week."

He didn't care.

"Bob, we're going to do this, you know we are," Rick said. "You just have to do this. It's just part of the drill."

That made all my fear go away and we did it. Rick has been my swim buddy ever since.

A few days after the last day of school in June 1972, we pulled on our backpacks and headed east. We took the bus from Tehran to Mashhad, where most of the traffic from the Orient Express, the train from Istanbul to Tehran, dropped off the Europeans on the Hippie Trail. We hitched a ride with a couple of Irish Hippies in a VW van to give us a ride to the Iranian side of the border and then got another ride in the back of an old Mercedes sedan over the ten miles of no-man's-land to the Afghan side and walked through customs.

Now in Afghanistan, we stuck our thumbs out, looking for anyone headed for Herat, an oasis city and the third-largest city in Afghanistan. It's the capital of Herat Province in the fertile valley of the Hari River in the western part of the country. The city was built along the Silk Road and had deep Persian influences, earning the nickname Little Iran.

It was interesting, although in Afghanistan where the premier language was Pashto or Dari, Herat was really a microcosm of Iran. More Farsi speakers were there than anywhere else. The language, architecture, culture, food, and just about everything else seemed to me to be more of a suburb of Tehran. As we traveled through Afghanistan this would become evidently clear how different this city was from the rest of the country. They were clearly accustomed to western hitchhikers as young peddlers were always trying to sell hashish to you wherever you went.

After a few days of roaming the city, taking in the sites, the food, and the people, we found a truck heading southeast and jumped in the back. We were headed to Kandahar along the not-completed Ring Road that sought to connect Kabul, Herat, Kandahar, and Mazar e Sharif, the largest cities in the country, and bring together the myriad of tribes, nationalities, and cultures that comprise the small landlocked country.

About a third of the way to Kandahar, the truck's engine started to sputter. Smoke leaked out from under the hood as it coasted to a halt on the side of the road. We all hopped out of the back of the truck as the driver tried to make repairs. It was soon clear to all of us the truck wasn't going to make it to Kandahar.

It was late afternoon, and the sun was sliding behind the mountains. We could head back to Herat and start again the next day or press onward and see if we could find a place to sleep. The group got together and decided to keep moving.

No one wanted to backtrack.

A few miles down the road, we found a beat-up taxi and squeezed inside. A compact Japanese sedan with tires, long worn away by the rugged Afghan roads, took us about halfway to Kandahar before the driver kicked us out. He wasn't headed to Kandahar and it was getting dark. We were in a little village area, really just a collection of biscuit-colored mud compounds. Not far from where he let us out, we saw a small mud compound and went over and knocked on the gate.

The gate strained against the hinges as it opened. The homeowner was a slight man with a thick black beard and baggy shirt that hung down to his knees. He smiled and gave me a curious look. It was clear he had no idea why an American teenager in jeans and a Mickey Mouse shirt was standing in front of his gate halfway between Kandahar and Herat.

Then I blew his mind when I asked him if we could sleep there in Farsi.

The Afghan was clearly a Pashtun and spoke Pashtu and luckily a smattering of Dari—a cousin of Farsi. It was enough that we could do basic communications. The Afghan people are gracious and generous. He didn't hesitate to offer his home and food.

"Come in," the Afghan said. "You can stay the night, but we need to lock you in our shed in back."

At first, I thought something got lost in translation. He wanted to lock us in the shed. We were a little concerned. Was this Afghan keeping us as hostages?

"Why?" I asked.

"Bandits," the Afghan said, pantomiming a rifle with his hands. "We have to invite them into our home as a courtesy, but they won't go through our sheds and stuff and you would be safe there," the Afghan said.

I looked back at the group and shrugged. I was met with the same. We didn't really have a choice. It was this or sleeping outside where the bandits—if they existed—could get us.

The shed was inside the compound but away from the main house. Inside, there was a dirt floor and shelves. From the smells it was clear that it was used as a temporary holding area for errant animals. We could sympathize with them and hoped for a different fate.

After a dinner of stewed meat, flatbread, and freshly chopped vegetables, we shuffled into the shed and set up camp. Outside, we heard the Afghan snap the lock shut. A couple of my friends poked around with their flashlights, looking for a means of escape, but failed. There was no way out that we could find. We'd know in the morning if this was a bad idea and had a problem. We all climbed into sleeping bags and soon I only heard the soft breathing of my sleeping friends.

I woke when a stream of light shone through the small windows in the shed. The coolness of the night had melted away and now the air inside the shed was humid, sauna-like. Soon after sunrise, we heard the Afghan outside the door opening the lock. He greeted us with a hearty hello and smile. Breakfast was waiting. On the way to a rug, where plates of fruit and bread were set out, I asked the Afghan if any bandits showed up.

"We did have visitors," he said. "It was a good thing we had you in the shed, not that they would do anything to you, but they might try to extract some money or something from you."

Then he laughed.

I am not the only person who has benefited from the kindness of the Afghan people. Marcus Luttrell, known as the Lone Survivor, also encountered a hugely courageous act of generosity during one of his missions that went terribly wrong in 2005. He was working alongside three other SEALs to hunt down Ahmad Shah, a leader associated with the Taliban when the team was ambushed by the Taliban.

One of his comrades literally died in his arms from a bullet wound to the head while another was blown up by a grenade while they hid together. The third SEAL was killed trying to establish a call for help. When a US helicopter carrying a support team arrived, the Taliban blew them out of the sky with a rocket-propelled grenade.

In the end, nineteen Americans died, and no one knew that Marcus was still alive. Marcus was truly alone, with a broken back and several bullet wounds. He tried to crawl his way to safety but found himself surrounded by another group of Afghan men. Marcus was wary of their intentions, but the men promised that they were not part of the Taliban. They offered to help him. With no other options, Marcus let the men carry him to their village where they kept him hidden from the Taliban until they could get a note to a Marine outpost that Marcus was alive and needed help. Despite threats from the Taliban to their own lives, the people of this village protected Marcus, like our host.

We joined our host for the morning meal. About an hour later, we were back on the Ring Road with our thumbs up.

The whole trip was an endeavor in trust.

When we got to Kandahar, we found a guesthouse and just wandered the city. From Kandahar, we took the bus to Kabul, where we stayed for a couple of weeks. I would climb up one of the mountains that ring the Afghan capital with an old man whose job it was to fire a cannon at noon every day. The Afghans used it to set their clocks. He was happy to have company. For us, it was a great adventure.

Kabul was just so lively. We bumped into a lot of hippies from the United States and Western Europe. A guy opening a clothing shop. Others had cafes or flop houses. We got cold beer at the Gandamack and spent an afternoon listening to Led Zeppelin and Pink Floyd. It was a really big mix of cultures and nations in Kabul. We fit right in and it just reaffirmed what we all believed. That you had to get out and be a part of the other cultures and societies and see how others see things.

From Kabul, we headed east to the Khyber Pass. We almost ran into the same fate as the British when we got accosted by a group of bandits after crossing into Pakistan. About five skinny men in baggy pants and long shirts blocked our path at gun-point. They had aged, long-barreled rifles that appeared to be more muskets than any current weapon, so it came across as more intimidating than life-threatening. They hinted at violence, but no one believed them. The bandits wanted to see everything we had, so we opened our backpacks. They hoped to find money, but we didn't have enough to make it worth their while. In fact, they seemed to take pity on us.

"You have nothing to take," said the leader, a middle-aged man who seemed to be a father figure to his younger colleagues. "You want to have lunch?"

We agreed. It was better than being mugged. We gathered off the road on a blanket and ate rice and chicken and bread and talked about America. It was a common theme everywhere we went. Few, if any, had ever come in contact with Americans, but all had great respect and admiration for it. They asked questions and we did our best to answer. It was nothing personal; it's just what they did.

I ate a lot of meals on blankets with my hands. I had a lot of conversations about America. I asked a lot of questions about Afghanistan, Pakistan, and eventually India. Each encounter, each day, I learned the same important lesson.

It's all about people—how you relate with them, how you talk to them, and at the end of the day, how you find common ground. It didn't matter where we were from or what language we spoke. That common ground came out at the compound between Kandahar and Herat and in the Khyber Pass over chicken and rice after an aborted mugging. That's really what this trip reinforced.

By the time we got to India, we were running out of time. We doubled back quickly. On the bus ride from Kabul to Kandahar, I had to use the bathroom. I was suffering from amoebic dysentery and was violently ill. I was about to blow chunks from both ends.

"You got to stop," I said, begging the bus driver. "I've got to get off this bus."

But the bus driver refused.

"No, we'll be there in just a minute."

"No, you don't understand."

But the bus driver wasn't going to stop. I returned to my seat.

I was clutching my gut. The diarrhea and nausea came in waves. For most of the ride, I was doubled over trying to hold everything down. The bus finally stopped at a small parking lot with cars and trucks lined up along the road. A squat mud outhouse for truck drivers and travelers sat near the parked trucks. Just inside the door were three holes in the ground with foot pads on either side. Two men squatted over the holes, leaving only the middle one open. I barely got my pants down before I was blowing shit all over the walls while I threw up into the hole. The other Afghans pulled up their pants and evacuated. Soon it was only me in there, suffering. When I finally recovered, I stumbled out of the outhouse into the warm midday sun.

"Where are you from?" said one of the Afghans who fled my outburst.

"Germany," I said in Pashtu.

I didn't want to be the ugly American who just destroyed their outhouse. When we got to Kandahar, I checked into a guest house. I was so bad off, we had to stay for a week to recover because it was coming out both ends all day long.

It took us two and a half months to go to India and back and I returned to Tehran exhausted but having learned many important lessons.

Take every opportunity, and people are good—everywhere. Just as important, they all liked us. Once they knew I was

American, the standard response centered on, "Please have dinner with us," "Would you like a goat?" or "Would you marry our daughter?" I believe the Afghanistan we invaded in 2001 was not much different, but we really never took the time or effort to find out. What I do know is that many of the early confrontations we were involved in 2001 resulted in no gunfire or casualties.

You hear a lot of people say never volunteer—when you go in the military never volunteer because you're going to get the shit job—well, that's an opportunity. If you're volunteering, the person asking is going to be indebted, but you also get to do something no one else will do because no one was willing to do it.

Think about that.

And it plays out in a lot of different realms. I'll give you one example. Coming out of the Naval War College in Newport, Rhode Island, I got a call about a week or two before leaving and it was Admiral Ray Smith, Commander, Naval Special Warfare.

"Hey, Bob, I want you to go down to Fort Bragg and interview with the new four-star who's going to run SOCOM."

General Wayne Downing was at another command at Fort Bragg but was about to take over SOCOM in Tampa. SOCOM is responsible for training and equipping all Special Operations Forces, including Navy SEALs. It is the higher headquarters responsible for managing the forces, but not a war-fighting entity. JSOC are the warriors.

"Oh, no, sir, I don't want to do that," I said. "I have orders for JSOC."

The line went quiet for a few minutes.

"Bob, I wasn't asking you," Smith said. "I was telling you. You're going down to do this interview."

I flew down on a C-12. From Pope Air Force Base, they drove me over to his office. I came in and he waved me over to a seat across from his desk. He talked for about fifteen minutes about the job and what he wanted to do, and he finally wanted to know my questions.

"Sir, if you make me do this job, how long would I have to do it for?"

Downing laughed.

"About a year because I will burn you out," he said.

"Okay," I said. "When do you make your decision?"

Downing looked at me, puzzled. "I have made my decision," he said. "You're my aide. Show up in Tampa in two weeks."

It ended up being the most wonderful experience. I learned more in that job than any other previous job I had. He was like a father to me and I got six hundred freefall jumps, including a landing on an aircraft carrier underway.

Who gets to do that shit?

Me, because I said yes. My whole career was like that. When no one else would do it, they'd call me. I was a journeyman in the SEAL community. Every year or two I was doing a different job, or I was somewhere else, but the experience and knowledge I gleaned from that paid dividends each and every day and added to every new adventure I was on. Saying yes for me meant going down a new path. I was always in it for the adventure.

I think that's what separates businesses, teams, and organizations, especially if you're looking at entrepreneurs. Do as much as you can. Take advantage of different adventures and opportunities.

Go do it.

I never regretted it, even in that Afghan outhouse.

CHAPTER 5

We Are All Accountable for Ourselves and to Others

We're underway off the coast of Chile and I'm the officer of the deck on mid-watch—midnight to four in the morning.

It's September 1983 and we're transiting from Peru to Chile. The task force is made up of about a half dozen ships from the US, Peru, and Chile and is steaming due south at twelve knots. It's about 2:30 in the morning and I'm on the bridge wing trying to stay alert after a rowdy port call and a full day's work.

After trying my hand as a pilot, I'd found my place driving ships like my father. I still wanted to be a SEAL but being on the bridge felt a hell of a lot more comfortable than being in a cockpit. Being part of the crew was a master class in the Gouge. We were a tight-knit family who incessantly interacted and worked closely together, twenty-four hours a day, seven days a week, 365 days a year. We depended on each other and looked after each other. I knew why my father loved this life.

Since boarding the USS *Scott* (a Kidd-class destroyer ordered by the Shah of Iran from my father but was undelivered due to the change of leadership in Iran associated with the Iranian Revolution) I'd felt at home and tonight I was the officer of the deck (OOD). I was responsible and accountable for the 325 people who lived on this ship during my watch. In this case, four hours of staying on course through the South Pacific Ocean.

I was on the bridgewing looking at the stars. It was a nice night. I scanned the ships ahead of us and listened for the Combat Information Center (CIC) to help me maintain position relative to the other ships and our assigned course and speed. If something came up, it was their job to inform me because they got it on their radar scopes way before I saw it. We were a formation of six ships, where each ship was assigned a location relative to each other, while all the ships maintained the same course and speed. I, and the rest of the bridge watch team, could see the running lights of other ships in the task force.

Ships display certain lights dictated by the law of the sea. You have a white bow and stern light. A red light on your left (port) side and a green light on the right (starboard) side. The lights allow a sailor to see which way a ship is traveling and at what angle. For example, if you see a white light with a red light in the middle, that means you're looking 45 degrees at that ship. If you see only a white light, that means you're looking at it head-on or at the stern. Combining this information with your radar readings allowed you to confirm that each ship was maintaining its assigned position, while the whole formation remained on the same course and speed to reach the desired location of the transit together.

There were two miles of separation between each ship. Standing on the bridgewing, I scanned forward, where I saw the white stern light of the ship in front of me and then turned to look off the starboard bow. I spotted three lights in a triangle—white at the top. Green on the left. Red on the right. I couldn't see the ship, only the lights. It took a second for my brain to kick in.

"Fuck me, those lights aren't right," I said under my breath. "She's coming right at us."

When you're doing twelve knots, two miles isn't a big gap. When another ship changes course, both vessels close very quickly. I'd missed the lights. The guys in the combat information center missed the ship on their scopes. I only caught it at the last moment and now we had to act before we collided. I dashed onto the bridge.

"Hard left rudder!" I said, telling the helmsman to turn the rudder all the way to the left.

"Hard left rudder, aye, sir," he said, throwing the wheel to the port side.

I felt the ship keel over to the port side as the bow started to track to the left. I raced out to the bridgewing. A destroyer was bearing down on us. I looked toward the bow and saw the gap between our ship and the destroyer shrinking rapidly. It was going to be close.

I could feel the ship. Its Peruvian bridge crew was scrambling too. They turned hard to port just in time to avoid a collision. Another second, and we would have crashed, no doubt killing sailors on both vessels and possibly sinking the multi-million-dollar destroyers. I stayed on the bridgewing and watched them pass. They were so close, it felt like I could reach across and touch them. The Peruvian ship had an engine problem and had turned to head back to port.

Unlucky for us, (me and the entire crew), the combat information center had missed it on the radar. We narrowly avoided a collision. But in doing so, I dumped half the crew out of their bunks, including the captain. He immediately arrived on the bridge more than upset! Rightfully so in that if we had even touched the other ship, he probably would have been relieved of command, and my naval career would have been over. We spent the rest of the watch completing an after-action debrief. At the end of all of it was all kudos to the bridge team. Combat didn't pick them up on radar and the old man had their ass for it.

The bad part of it was the captain now had complete trust and confidence in me, so a month later he wanted me as the officer of the deck as we went through the Strait of Magellan. We were the deepest draft ship to transit it at the time and as we entered the strait, I saw the remnants of other ships that had run aground navigating this challenging waterway.

I did everything in my power to keep the ship safe. I checked the plot provided by our radars. I had sailors on the bridge team incessantly shooting the angles from land-based known references. It was total concentration as we ran the transit.

In the middle of the strait, I got a call from the radio shack. They had a message that was important, and I needed to see it. I couldn't leave the bridge, so I told them to bring a hard copy to the bridge. A sailor showed up with a shit-eating grin and handed me a sheet of paper. I took it and glanced at it quickly. As I read it, I realized it was my orders to go to BUD/S or SEAL training. My dream was realized. I was going to be a US Navy SEAL. But seconds later, I was snapped back to the present and midway through a transit of the Strait of Magellan.

No mistakes, Harward.

I freaked out because I wanted to make sure the ship was on track and didn't run aground, screwing up my chances of going to SEAL training.

I was responsible and accountable for the safety and well-being of that ship and all those people. And that lesson stuck with me throughout my career, even when I made it to the teams. I didn't care if I was a platoon commander or a SEAL team captain in command of all the teams on the West Coast; I felt responsible and accountable for all the people under my charge. To give you another example, it was considered standard form at a SEAL team when someone met their qualifications to be a range safety officer or running a dive or parachute jump to just sign off. You'd get a stack of forms and the captain—confident the SEAL was trained—signed off.

That wasn't enough for me.

I called in each SEAL and before I'd sign the form, I'd make sure they understood what the qualification meant and what I expected of them.

"Hey, look, you are personally responsible and accountable when I sign this letter," I told each one. "If you're on that range, or you're conducting that jump or you're conducting that dive and someone gets hurt or injured, I'm coming after you."

I'd usually pause to let that sink in. To me, this wasn't something you just checked off. This was more than that. By getting the qualification, they agreed to the responsibility of taking care of their teammates and making sure everyone was safe and lived up to the standard. If something went wrong, they failed in their responsibility.

"You're going to be held accountable for it," I told them.

It must have worked because I never got anyone hurt or killed on my watch. Stressing accountability at each and every step of the way paid huge dividends. Because of that, when someone wasn't accountable in my command, they suffered my wrath.

I had several no-notice six-month deployments when I was in command of SEAL Team THREE, which meant the team had to run on its own without my leadership. For the most part, the team performed exceptionally, except once.

I had just gotten back to the Team area and was working out outside when a young kid—he looked like a college student with a lean swimmer's physique—came up and started talking to me.

"Sir, I'm one of the midshipmen stashed at your command for a month as part of my midshipman training."

"I didn't know that," I said, seeing that I had been deployed for much of my command tour.

Midshipmen from the Naval Academy and Reserve Officer Training Corps units across the country shipped their students to ships and commands across the Navy in the summer. The goal was to give midshipmen real-world experience and training. Give them a taste of life and show them what they were signing up to do once they got to the fleet. It was also a chance to try out different careers to see where you might want to serve.

But the midshipmen we got at the SEAL command already knew where they wanted to serve.

"Well, sir," the midshipman said. "I'd like to get my jump wings."

Midshipmen are authorized for airborne training. They make five static line jumps to get qualified. If he could get five more at the SEAL team, he would earn the right to wear gold jump wings on his uniform. It's a big deal for new guys coming into the community. It's another badge on their uniform and it shows they're not a new guy. They've done something.

But it wasn't going to happen at my command. I explained to the midshipman that he wasn't on jump orders. The midshipman shook his head. He told me the command let another midshipman jump while I was deployed.

"What?" I said.

"Yeah," the midshipman said. "He went and conducted a freefall."

I was angry.

"There's no way," I said. "Come with me."

We ran to my office. I called my command master chief, the top enlisted soldier in the command, my operations officer, and my air operations chief, who oversaw all the jumps.

"Hey, what's going on here? This kid said that we let some kid do a freefall?"

No one had an answer or knew anything about this midshipman conducting a freefall jump.

"Well, let's find out," I said.

By lunch, I found out the midshipman who wasn't assigned to the team and wasn't on jump orders got a freefall jump with our SEAL team. One of my SEALs, a good operator, was dating the sister of this midshipman. The midshipman was civilian freefall-qualified through the United States Parachute Association—meaning he could go and jump at a civilian airport—but he wasn't qualified in the eyes of the Navy. The midshipman showed up at the jump brief having been invited by a SEAL. While sitting in on the jump brief, the chief who was running the operation didn't notice the midshipman had signed his name on the manifest.

Easy to understand, as this was a jump supporting numerous SEAL teams, so it would be common for the chief running the evolution not to know everyone. However, when the midshipman signed the manifest, certifying he was qualified, he violated Navy policy and guidance by fraudulently attesting to his qualifications for high-risk training, and the chief failed in his responsibilities to verify the qualification. It was also clear to me the midshipman violated the US Naval Academy honor code because he didn't tell the truth.

At the drop zone, someone gave the midshipman a parachute. He put it on and got checked out by the chief, who made sure he put the equipment on correctly. During the check, the chief asked the midshipman if he was qualified.

"Yeah, I'm qualified," he said. "I'm good to go."

He got on the plane, and he jumped safely. If he had been hurt, I probably would've been relieved from command. When I confronted the chief in my office after finding out about the jump, he shrugged.

"Well, sir, the kid told me he was civilian freefall-qualified."

Wrong answer, and one I didn't take lightly.

"No, chief, I signed your jumpmaster letter," I said, reminding him of his certification letter. "You didn't know this guy. How did you know he was qualified?"

There was no answer.

The chief knew he messed up. I took the chief and SEAL who invited the midshipman to the jump to captain's mast. In the Navy, when you get in trouble, you go to captain's mast. It's a non-judicial process where commanders can administratively determine wrongdoing and mete appropriate punishments. While the penalty in this case had no lasting effects (as no one was hurt), this lapse in accountability could have cost people's lives and careers. I wanted to make an example to make sure it didn't happen again.

But the midshipman went back to the Naval Academy when this was all over. I could not take the midshipman to mast, so he got off without a punishment. But when I found out the midshipman was in town for leave, I got him into the command and confronted him. He denied telling the chief he was qualified and said he signed the manifest because everyone else did. That didn't cut it with me. There was nothing I could do to him directly, but I wrote a letter to the Naval Academy and—because this kid wanted to be a SEAL—made it clear we didn't want him.

"This isn't a kid we want," I wrote. "He was duplicitous in his actions, which could've resulted in him being hurt, but more importantly, it jeopardized the careers of two good SEALs who we have invested in for years, all so he could meet his own objective in saying he jumped with SEALs."

I sent the letter to the Naval Academy and to the detailer, who selects officers for the SEAL community. Neither one acted on it. I reckon it is because the midshipman was a star swimmer. That kept him at the academy and in the Navy, which disappointed me. They failed to hold this kid accountable for an honor violation. To add insult, the detailer still allowed the midshipman to be selected and go to BUD/S.

Fast forward a year later, this kid is going through BUD/S. I got called on another six-month deployment, but when I returned, I was running on the beach in San Diego and one of the SEAL instructors stopped me. We caught up on the latest and greatest around the community and then the instructor filled me in on the latest gossip from BUD/S.

"You heard about the tragedy?" he asked with a big grin, so I knew something was up.

"No."

The midshipman who'd lied about his jump qualification and who'd been shuttled into the SEALs because of his star-athlete status got dropped from BUD/S the week before graduation because of integrity issues. The instructors saw the same ethics problems I saw and even though he had made it through the course and met all the minimum standards, they dropped him and would not give him his SEAL trident the week before graduation.

The instructors held the midshipman—a Naval Officer by the time he got to training—accountable. While he met the physical standards, he failed ethically. He did not have the leadership skills. Unfortunately, a chief and another SEAL were accountable for the actions of this Naval Officer and paid the price for their lapse. But reinforcing accountability at every level and from every angle are the standards we all need and expect. The instructors were accountable to themselves and their community. They didn't turn a blind eye; instead they made the hard choice because that was the job, and they knew what a lapse in accountability does to the teams. I could not have been prouder of their actions.

Unfortunately, accountability is hard and difficult work and there are many examples of where the process fails.

A SEAL with many overseas deployments, including service in Iraq and Afghanistan, reportedly went rogue. He had a reputation as a hothead who liked to fight. Despite favorable evaluations from his commanders, he was investigated and cleared for shooting a girl in Afghanistan in 2010, and allegedly tried to run over a Navy security officer in 2014 during a traffic stop. Later in 2017 he was accused by his own team of violating the rule of war during the Battle of Mosul in Iraq, including the murder of a prisoner of war. The accusers claimed he stabbed a wounded teenage fighter from the Islamic State with his knife and then posed for photos with the body. Ultimately the Naval Criminal Investigation Service got involved and then arrested him. He was charged with premeditated murder, attempted murder and obstruction of justice. There were additional allegations that he threatened to kill his teammates if they reported his actions.

This SEAL "decided to act like the monster the terrorists accuse us of being," said the naval prosecutor. "He handed ISIS propaganda from heaven." Needless to say, the situation with the investigation, the media frenzy and the military messaging, much less political ramifications at the national level continued to spiral out of control, leading to a less than satisfactory conclusion for anyone, much less the individual.

It appears clear to me that the SEAL community failed this one, over numerous years. No one ever held this sailor accountable for his actions over many years, specifically over his career. The same Brotherhood that makes the SEAL community also failed the SEAL family in the most extreme way possible. The SEAL was never held accountable because no one was willing to, until it was too late, and with devastating ramifications. A failure of leadership at every level, which let it continue. Harming more people than it should have along the way. Many people and leaders in the community reportedly justified his actions by saying:

"He is a good guy."

"I know him."

"That was just a mistake."

If the stories are true, this sailor acted in war as he did in peace. He was a bully who used war as an excuse to brutalize a teenage prisoner. He convinced himself that the prisoner was no longer human. The SEAL traded his honor and the honor of his men and country to deliver a punishment.

The whole case was devoid of accountability. Everyone, over many years, avoided taking on the problem and finding a solution. It is similar to the midshipman conducting an unauthorized jump. Some would suggest they are oceans apart from each other, but not the way I see it. Lack of accountability is a slippery slope that is hard to stop once it festers itself in any organization or team.

Accountability and confrontation are aligned. If you're going to avoid confrontation, you'll never hold anyone accountable, and I see a lot of that in the business world. To really be successful, to reach the gold standard, you need both confrontation and accountability. You need to be able to harness, understand, and leverage confrontation in a constructive, productive manner as part of your accountability.

This SEAL was the antithesis of the Gouge. He burned his contract with humanity if he fired on innocent civilians and declared through his actions that he wasn't going to be accountable to himself, so why should we expect him to be accountable to his fellow SEALs? The only reason the system worked is because those below him challenged the responsibility and the accountability in not only him but all the others who were above him. Accountability comes from below and above, and in some places, that's what makes it so challenging and difficult.

But we've created cultural accountability problems in part because of social media. Tweeting. Posting on Facebook. All of these sites put a barrier between human connection, allowing people to refuse accountability for what they're saying or doing.

At the end of the day, social media is both good and bad. In fact, I'm a supporter because it is a vehicle to pass *good Gouge*. It is a connector. It is a platform to make sure people stay informed, but the problem is by nature, social media acts as a mirror. It reflects our culture. It reinforces your accountability to yourself. And in some regards, it reinforces the best of us.

But my main concern with social media is you can be anonymous.

I think it takes accountability away from people and they don't have to own what they say. The lack of accountability is why social media can be a toxic place. It is why people throw out racist, sexist, and violent threats because they know little will stick. These are things that no one would say face-to-face. Accountability is a tough business. But the best leaders know how to effectively implement it to get the best results for their team so they can fulfill their purpose.

CHAPTER 6

Faith in People Is My Religion

For the Gouge to work, you need a little faith. This isn't faith in something unseen. It's taking stock of the man or woman next to you and having faith they are going to do what needs to be done for the common good.

I've always had faith in the chain that connects society. That human need for community. It is a building block of the Gouge, but more than that, it is essential because if you don't have faith in one another, there is no trust, no passing of information or guidance, and the whole system breaks down.

Very few men earned my faith as quickly as Jim Mattis. It all started with my boss at Special Operations Command Pacific (SOCPAC). He hated going to the Commander-in-Chief morning staff meeting. He was an Air Force Brigadier General and the meeting was dominated by the Navy and Marine Corps' most senior military officers (Admirals and Generals). My Air Force boss thought we would have better access and relationships by having me (a Naval SEAL officer) attending the meetings.

It was July 1999 and I was a captain but was sitting next to flag officers. I seemed to always find a spot near Lieutenant General Michael Hagee. These meetings went on for a couple of years and Hagee and I ended up becoming friends and workout buddies until we all got new assignments.

I left Hawaii in August 2001 for San Diego. I was replacing Bill McRaven—who would go on to lead the Bin Laden raid—as Group One commander responsible for all the West Coast SEALs. Hagee left at the same time to become Marine division commander up in Camp Pendleton, which sits between Los Angeles and San Diego. We weren't far from one another, and Hagee told me he'd come down for a visit once we both got settled into our new commands.

It was late August 2001 when I got his call. I'd been in San Diego for a couple of weeks talking to people and getting the lay of the land before I took command from McRaven, which was going to happen on the last day of the month.

"Hey, Bob," Hagee said. "I've heard you guys are doing some neat stuff. Can I come down and spend the day with you?"

I can't really say no to a general, plus he was a good dude, and I wanted an excuse to catch up with him. Plus, it gave me something to do while I waited to take over.

"Oh, sure," I said. "Come on down, sir."

Hagee and some of his staff drove down from Pendleton and we gave him the Gucci tour. We showed him all the cool toys—boats, weapons, vehicles. All the stuff that says we're Special Operations. We also ran him through our operations and support capabilities. A great day overall. He went back impressed, I think, but more importantly, with a better understanding of our abilities.

The next day, I got a call. It was Hagee again. I figured it was to say thanks, but he had another request.

"Hey, Bob," he said. "I got this new one-star general. His name is Jim Mattis. Will you show him around like you showed me?"

Suddenly, I was the Marine Corps' favorite tour guide. But we're all brothers in the same service and I never passed up a chance to show off what the boys could do.

"Well, sure, sir," I said. "Yeah, OK. Send him my way."

Mattis came down with some staff and we redid the tour. Boats. Weapons. Capabilities. By the end of it, I was ready to go back to BUD/S and do it all over again rather than do another tour.

Mattis, like Hagee, turned out to be another great guy. Smart. Asked all the right questions. I could see his mind working, plugging us into his battle plans in the event we were called to action. At the end of the day, off he went, I think, feeling the same way Hagee did.

With my tour guide duties complete, I took command on the last day of August 2001. Bill McRaven—on crutches because he broke his pelvis in a parachute accident—was headed to Washington. Luckily, I had arranged for him to go work at the White House with Wayne Downing, my old boss from SOCOM. Downing retired and went to the White House. Downing wanted me to go work for him, but I was taking command.

"Well, you know anyone else?" Downing said.

"Hell yes, Bill McRaven," I said.

That's how we got our foot into the White House. Bill went and worked for Downing and then I followed. But not before I deployed to Afghanistan because eleven days after I took command, al Qaeda terrorists crashed four planes—two into the World Trade Center, one into the Pentagon and another into a Pennsylvania field after some brave Americans refused to allow them to carry out their plans.

Before the smoke dissipated from lower Manhattan, I was on a plane with my command group and SEAL teams headed for Bahrain. That is where we staged before heading into Afghanistan. As we waited for the teams and gear to arrive, I started planning. We were slated to enter Afghanistan from the south and operate around Helmand and Kandahar provinces. I knew the area well. The irony wasn't lost on me that I'd hitchhiked my way through the area as a kid and now I was invading it as a SEAL. But the area was also immensely important because the Taliban was born in Kandahar and it was their stronghold. Taking their heartland was operational and strategically important if we were going to root out al Qaeda and topple the government that protected them.

I was planning for a fight. This was our first war in a long time. We'd trained for combat, but most, if not all, of my guys did not have any combat experience. We were in uncharted waters in a landlocked country, and we were somewhat on our own. The mission was simple. Lead my SEALs into Afghanistan. But the details were hard.

How do we get there?

How do we get resupplied?

Once in Afghanistan, where do I set up a base?

Who protects that base?

How do I evacuate the wounded?

Between planning sessions, I took breaks. I liked to walk to clear my head. The base in Bahrain was busy around the clock as the US military surged supplies and equipment in anticipation of the invasion. After a long planning session, I was outside of the operations center getting air. It was pitch black and I was standing out under a light when I heard a familiar voice.

"Hey, Bob. Bob Harward, is that you?"

I turned and could just make out the silhouette of a man. He was lean with short hair. Obviously a Marine. Then, everything clicked. It was Jim Mattis from my tour. We'd met several weeks earlier in San Diego. He worked for Hagee.

"Bob, what are you doing here?" Mattis said, shaking my hand.

I wanted to ask him the same question.

"Well, sir, I'm taking the SEALs into Afghanistan," I told him.

Mattis, now under the light, smiled.

"I'm taking the Marines," he said, pausing for a minute, the germ of an idea forming in his head. A seed was planted during our tour in San Diego. It was almost like he was recounting his tour and all the ways we'd talked about mission alignment. Somewhere in his brain, the kernel of an idea lived and he found it that night in Bahrain.

"Hey, you want to go together?"

The offer was too good to be true. A big unit like the Marines solved a lot of my headaches. He had a long logistical tail and could keep my smaller, leaner force supplied and protected, allowing me to flex my resources into operations.

"Shit, sounds good," I said.

Mattis stuck out his hand and we shook on it. That was it. From the moment we made the deal, we were interlocked and ran the invasion of Afghanistan from the south. The first guys on the ground in scale.

A day later, I met Mattis at his headquarters to figure out the details.

"I got permission," he told me. "We're going in. Let's go in tomorrow. Are you ready?"

We were, or at least I thought we were. Maybe more ambition than reality.

"OK, sir."

Our staff got together and planned while I called back to Special Operations Command Central, my higher command. When I told them we were headed in, their answer was no. It wasn't my decision to make. They wanted to know my arrangement with Mattis. The staff in Tampa was freaking out, but I didn't have time to waste. I pushed back and around and around we went. All the while, after the handshake, I knew we were going. There was no way I was going to let Mattis down.

"Hey, guys," I said after getting the runaround from the staff for the last time. "Where's the boss? He's got to tell me that I can't go."

The Chief of Staff didn't have an answer.

"We can't get hold of him. He's running around with the agency somewhere."

I wasn't waiting.

"Well, then I'm going, guys," I said. "If you find him and he wants to stop me, tell him to call me, but if not, I'm going."

I killed the line. No way I was going to pass up a chance to ride in with the Marines. After a couple of joint planning sessions, it was clear neither one of us had the capabilities to do it alone, but together we were a perfect match. Mattis was the easy button personified and I offered him a joint task force of Special Operations Units from not only the United States but Canada, Germany, Australia, Great Britain, and more.

The next day, my guys flew into Pakistan using our Special Operations aircraft and did a hydrographic reconnaissance of the beaches to make sure the Marines could offload their equipment (just as SEALs were originally conceived and built for in World War II at Normandy and for the Pacific Campaign). Next, we put guys on the ground outside of Kandahar for forty-eight hours to ensure we had a secure forward operating base we could use before guiding the Marines in with our Special Operations helicopters.

With the Marines on the ground, we set up a base of operations and started raiding targets in Helmand and Kandahar before taking the city. It was a brilliant marriage of capabilities, enabled by this trust and belief in each other and mutual support based on his leadership.

I was technically working for the Special Operations component of CENTCOM, which oversaw all American Special Operations Forces in the Middle East. He was technically working for the Navy component of CENTCOM. We leveraged those two relationships. You know, "Mom said no, so let's go to Dad." If my command said no, we just pivoted to his chain of command and vice versa.

"Hey, Bob, you get this thing approved. I'll work this part."

All the while, I worked directly with Mattis. Here he was, a flag officer, a general, and I was still just a captain. Most of the time those kinds of relations are very one-sided. The general gives an order, and the captain does it. That is how the military worked. From the handshake in Bahrain, it was Jim and Bob. He still gave the orders, and I still executed them, but there was mutual respect and faith that each of us was doing our job to achieve the mission. This faith in one another permeated up and down the chain of command in everything we did, and I think it was the number one attribute of our success.

It was strange because I didn't have a history with him. I met the man one day for four hours. But in those four hours we were together, we confirmed the trust and belief in each other and people in general. If you want to call that a relationship, fine. He impressed me with his humility and unbridled confidence, he seemed like a great guy, and for some strange reason, he seemed to have a lot of faith in me. We both understood one another and when it came time to work together, we had faith in one another's abilities and character.

That faith is integral for the Gouge to work. You must trust and believe in one another. It's different than what most people think of faith. This isn't religious faith because that is predicated on trusting the unprovable. This faith is placed in the bond between two people, casting your lot with your fellow man in hopes of achieving a common goal.

Faith was something I learned through the Gouge. My family didn't really go to church. The Gouge kind of became my religion, but that doesn't mean I didn't have faith. Growing up in a Muslim country, I learned faith through the eyes of Muhammad's followers. The morning call to prayer. The hustle and bustle of the mosque on Fridays. There is no escaping God in the Middle East, especially among the Muslims who are fond of blaming everything from a late bus to war on God's will.

Inshallah.

God willing, something will happen.

I believe there's someone, but I don't really believe in a religion of one over the other. If you want to be a Buddhist, I'll tell you, more power to you. If you want to be a Catholic, more power to you. If you want to be a Muslim, more power to you. That's all fine. But every now and then, I did get proof of the faith of a bigger kind, of not the people on this planet, but whoever God or Allah or Buddha, whoever that is, I've gotten proof of that. I'm the goddamn luckiest person in the world, or someone's helping me along the way. And everyone I know has told me they don't know anyone who's got more holly up their ass than me. I think it comes from how I treat other people and the things I do.

I grew up with more faith in people than religion. Every good deed I did for someone they returned in kind. Anything people did for me, I tried to do good for them as opposed to religion, which was nebulous. I never could really touch or get proof of a higher power. My faith in people has proven correct, that is the proof I needed in a higher power. If I went into every relationship believing that we're all trying to do our best, then I got better results than if I went in skeptical or cynical. Trust but verify, but, you know, trust.

With most people, verification comes naturally.

Remember, they're all sharing their experiences to help each other be smarter than the situation they're in. That could be in warfighting or just everyday life. But that sharing of the Gouge is that contract we all have with one another. Earth is really no different than a destroyer floating alone in the sea.

We're all in this together.

General James N. Mattis, former US Secretary of Defense. Jim lives by the value and ethos of the Gouge, as good as any man could, leading by example. I feel fortunate to have followed in his footsteps throughout my career and it is an honor and a privilege to be his Swim Buddy.

CHAPTER 7

Never Quit, but Saying No Is Always an Option

I was taught early on that there was no ringing the bell.

No matter how much things sucked, never quit. Never stand up and stagger over to the ship's bell and ring it.

In the SEAL community, quitting is a mortal sin.

The training is considered some of the hardest in the world with the highest attrition rates of all military training. The Navy always beats us up about it because we start with a class of 130 or more and by the end, we give the fleet back ninety to a hundred sailors, costly in time and resources as it is repeated every few months.

Before BUD/S, everyone is looking for the best Gouge to make it through. But the best advice I got, and give, is don't quit. No matter how hard it is. No matter how much they demand of you. No matter how hypothermic you get. Make it to the end of the evolution. Make it to the next meal. Make it to the end of the day.

But the instructors know that is the Gouge, so they're going to encourage you to ring the bell, signaling you've given up. You'll be freezing—hypothermic in the surf and they'll stand on the dry sand and deliver a monologue about hot pizza, warm beds, and uninterrupted sleep. They'll talk you into believing that the good life is one ring away. The ones who make it through refuse to quit. Once inculcated into this philosophy, they never quit. That mindset that got them through the training is the same mindset that allows the Navy to keep them for life. On the plus side our retention after becoming a SEAL is one of the highest across all the military forces; the more important attribute and benefit of this renowned difficult program and the attributes it inculcates and reinforces. These same people go through this incredibly hard career and spend thirty years in the Navy until they're forced to retire. Look at me. I was in for forty years and up until my last assignment was still deploying with no notice.

But quitting gets a bad rap. People think of laziness. No confidence. Failure. Quitting in BUD/S is one thing, but the reality is quitting—especially in the civilian world—shows optimism about the future. An eagerness to do something new. A confidence that if you jump ship, you won't drown but rather just land in a better boat.

Take Chris Cassidy.

He was with me in Afghanistan and led some of the toughest operations. Chris was a first-class SEAL and one of our best officers. Well, after returning from our deployment, he came into my office in San Diego and told me he was leaving the SEALs. I was floored. Why would he want to leave, especially now, when we are in a position to do what we always trained and prepared for? We were going to be running and gunning for years to come.

This was the big show, especially for SEALs. He knew it, and that is what was driving his decision. It was too hard on his family, both the deployments and uncertainty if he would eventually come home, like many of his teammates, who had not.

"Well, look, if you're going to do this, you should stay in the reserves," I said.

Cassidy shook his head.

"I'm not getting out of the Navy," he said. "I'm just going to do something else in the Navy."

That brought out my smirk.

"What the hell are you going to do?"

I'd spent time in the fleet before I joined the SEALs, and while valuable, it wasn't the same job or culture. As I said above, BUD/S does a good job of weeding out non-SEALs. Our culture often doesn't mix well with others.

"I think I'm going to be an astronaut," he said.

"Oh yeah, right," I said. "You think you're a frickin' rocket scientist or something?"

Now Cassidy smirked.

"Well, sir, I am a rocket scientist."

I wanted to launch across the table to choke him for directly reinforcing his superior intellect and education, but he had a valid point. I resigned myself to the fact he was leaving.

"Sir, I want to be an astronaut," Cassidy said. "Will you write the endorsement for me?"

"Of course," I told him and wrote a glowing endorsement, as he is absolutely top-notch in every fashion.

After he left my office and the SEALs, he went on to join NASA and later SpaceX. He's been to space four times and is the lead trainer for all the astronauts. His quitting the SEAL community was just an opportunity to say yes to something else. Remember, no means yes. That is after you get past quitting. In fact, the one time I quit, I landed in a better boat.

Right before I graduated from the Naval Academy in 1979, I had to pick my warfare specialty. There were three to choose from and special warfare or SEALs were not options. I could join the fleet as a surface warfare officer and drive ships, aviation and fly jets, or nuclear power and serve on submarines or the engine room of a carrier. Marines was not an option for me as they appeared a little too regimented and disciplined for me. Since I couldn't be a SEAL, I went to flight school.

But no one thought I was a pilot.

Your classmates write the bio under your picture in the Naval Academy yearbook. Mine said something like, "Bob Harward toyed with the idea of nuclear subs, but he was kidding. He is going to flight school, but we all know his real heart and where he should be is in the Navy SEALs. But we just don't know if the SEAL community is ready for Bob."

I agreed with them, but my hands were tied. I was a midshipman without a home. There was no direct path to the SEALs. Before making my warfare selection, I hit up my classmates and father, looking for some Gouge. Submarines didn't appeal to me. Learning nuclear power is hard and being underwater for months at a time had no appeal. I need to run and swim. I needed to be outside. It was either surface warfare, like my father, or aviation.

Everyone pointed me toward aviation. It was a much better lifestyle. You got to fly and it wasn't as hard a life as a surface warfare officer. But I got bum Gouge. All my information came from my classmates who wanted to be pilots. They were on the juice. Look, I get it. Flying jets gets the girls. Everyone looks cool in a flight suit. And for thrill seekers, little compares to breaking the sound barrier. I mean, it is hard not to be cool as a pilot.

But I hated flying.

It lacked imagination. It felt like a series of checklists. There was no art to it. It was too pedantic, like driving a bus. You got in a plane and went from point A to point B. We were training to repeat processes over and over and over. I'm going to take the jet out. I'm going to fly it around. I'm going to come back and land it.

Repeat. Repeat. Repeat. OK.

Plus, we were sitting around all the time. We'd brief and then sit. We'd fly and then come back and sit in the ready room. Checklists and meetings followed by way too much hurrying up and waiting. I was very physical. I liked running. I liked working out. None of that seemed to pay dividends in the aviation community. It didn't matter how many pushups I could do in the cockpit.

It didn't help I am ODD: organizational defiance disorder.

There isn't a bureaucracy or process I can't hate. It's something children grow out of at six or seven years old. I never grew out of it. Fighting the bureaucracy. Bucking the system. Going my own way was my North Star. It worked out for me for over forty years, but not when I got to flight training in Pensacola. I got through the ground school and completed a half dozen flights before I tapped out. There was no way I would stay in the Navy if I had to keep flying. I dropped my request to transfer.

"I don't think this lifestyle is for me," I told my instructor.

The instructors tried to dissuade me from doing it, but I just knew it wasn't for me. For the record, I wasn't Maverick, but I wasn't a bad pilot. I got good grades and the instructors encouraged me to stay.

The next step was figuring out what I was going to do in the Navy. They told me I couldn't be a SEAL without first completing another assignment. Submarines were out of the question. The goal was to find the quickest way.

"We'll send you to a ship," the detailer said.

"Can I be a SEAL from there?"

"If you earn your surface warfare pin, you can apply then."

The pin was awarded only after you learned everything about your ship, from the engineering spaces to the weapons, and, most importantly, driving the ship. The SWO (surface warfare officer) pin—like a pilot's wings—signified expertise.

"OK," I said.

I left flight school with no regrets. My Gouge was so bum that I found out two of my buddies who also wanted to be SEALs beat me to BUD/S because they went surface warfare, picked minesweepers, and earned their warfare pin in a year. They made it to the SEALs two years ahead of me. They had the Gouge!

I was taking the long way.

From Pensacola, I spent twenty-seven weeks in Newport, Rhode Island, and got assigned to a destroyer. The training was figurately and literally a homecoming. I was born in Newport and knew a lot about ship driving because of my father. I was more at home in the surface warfare community than I was in the pilot community. Once I got to the ship, no one cared that I'd started as a pilot. All they cared about was if I could do my job and take care of the ship and crew. But I learned a hard lesson. Being on a ship was hard. You're working with young kids. You're at sea all the time. I was married and I was gone a lot. It's a hard life, much harder than being a SEAL.

When I finally got to San Diego, BUD/S was like a holiday adventure camp. I got to be challenged. I got to do all the stuff that I had dreamed about and thought I would never get to do. It was just fun. Those guys on ships and planes, they're working their asses off. It's a tough career. It was dog-eat-dog. I have the utmost respect for them and really had great disdain for the SEALs who thought they were something special for being a SEAL. I thought some were pompous and didn't understand how good they had it when so many others serving had it so hard.

The caliber of young officers we attract to BUD/S and the SEAL community—like Chris Cassidy—are absolutely extraordinary, and the training only serves to validate they can do absolutely anything they want to do.

While working at the White House on the National Security Staff in 2004, I met Rick Nelson, another Naval Officer who considered himself to be a good racquetball player. Being somewhat competitive, I was always pushing him to play, yet he always found a work reason to avoid getting on the court with me. After a year he finally ran out of excuses and we played hooky one afternoon and matched up at Fort Myer.

I destroyed him in the first game.

In the second game, I was up fourteen to nil. I went for a power shot, and the next thing I heard was a pop. My bicep detached from my arm and was coiled up in my shoulder. Not a pretty sight.

Nelson was quick to claim victory, but I was having no part of it. I tried to continue the match with my left arm. Needless to say, I was not as proficient and as the pain magnified, I finally had to quit the match. When I got to the Bethesda naval hospital for the surgery to reattach my bicep, they put me on the table and quickly administered the painkiller for the operation. Just before going down for the count, the orthopedic came in. It was Lieutenant Commander Dan Valeck. As I was passing out, he reminded me that he had previously been a SEAL and had served for me on SEAL Team THREE as a platoon commander. I passed out, greatly concerned that I would wake up with my penis sewn to my forehead. Needless to say, he must have liked me at SEAL Team THREE, as the operation went well, and I was back to full fighting speed in short order. I was glad to know he had quit the SEAL community to move on to bigger and better things!

When I returned to the White House, there was a racquetball trophy on my desk designating me second place—loser—in the annual Nelson/Harward racquetball tournament. The son-of-a-bitch has yet to get back on a court with me.

All that to say, the SEAL methodology pounds the "never quit" mantra, but if you follow the Gouge it is going to challenge you to dig deep into what your purpose is and your contract with humanity. It's going to force you to live up to your maximum potential. Not everybody can be a SEAL, pilot, or ship driver. If you quit something, fine, move on to something else. It will just open other doors for you and those doors—in the case of Chris Cassidy, Dan Valeck, and me—are pretty damn good adventures. If I had stayed in aviation or ships, I never would've had the career I had.

Quitting doesn't end you. It starts you.

CHAPTER 8

Saying No Is Not Easy

General Jim Mattis called as soon as he accepted the Secretary of Defense post in the Trump Administration in 2016. He wanted to pick my brain about some of the civilian appointments he needed in the Pentagon.

He needed an Undersecretary of Defense for Intelligence and an Undersecretary of Defense for Policy. Mattis was trying to recruit me for a position. Meanwhile, Mike Flynn, who I served with in Afghanistan and Iraq, was serving as the National Security Advisor and wanted to talk.

To be clear, I was happy in the position I had transitioned to upon retiring from the Navy. Leading the Middle East business for a large defense company and living in Abu Dhabi was a great gig. But both Mattis and Flynn wanted to meet with me when I returned from UAE for an annual leaders meeting in Florida.

During my two days in Washington, DC, I talked to the National Security Council staff at the White House and Mattis' team at the Pentagon, giving them my opinion on China, Iran, and other security threats. All good conversations. After the meetings, I was headed to the airport to fly down to Florida to attend the annual business meeting when I got a call from Steve Bannon to come back to the White House. Bannon wouldn't tell me what he wanted to talk about, only that he wanted to meet me.

I told the driver to turn around and head back to the city. I got badged into the White House and ushered into a room with Bannon. He welcomed me back and we talked for a few minutes. After that he directed me to a conference room in the Old Executive Office Building, where a team of national security staffers waited. They interviewed me about my career and experience. They weren't picking my brain for advice, and I quickly realized I was being vetted. I figured Flynn wanted me on his staff, but I wasn't hot on the idea.

The meeting took an hour and Bannon saw me out. That was a Friday. I flew down to Orlando for the meeting the next day. The meeting started the following Monday, but everyone was arriving over the weekend. Bannon called me again on Sunday and asked that I come back to the White House on Monday.

"Why?" I said.

"We need to talk to you," he said. "Come back to the White House."

Bannon wanted me to meet with Reince Priebus, President Trump's chief of staff. He wouldn't take no for an answer. It must have been the military upbringing in me, but I couldn't say no. I told my bosses that I had to miss Monday's session to fly to Washington. The bosses wanted to know what the White House wanted, but I still had no idea. Before I arrived, news broke that Flynn was facing some issues for lying to the FBI and Vice President Mike Pence.

Monday morning, a car met me at the arrival terminal at Dulles and took me straight to the White House. Vice President Pence met me at the apron and took me into the residence. We walked into the Map Room and he and I talked for a few minutes. Bannon came in next with Jared Kushner. We were all sitting there talking when Mattis came in with President Trump.

Everyone popped tall. Trump spotted me and we shook hands. We made some small talk for a few minutes, nothing pressing or newsworthy. President Trump seemed to have something on his mind and I got a sense he was trying to get a sense of me. Could we work together? Could he trust me? It was a sniff test. Finally, President Trump turned to Bannon.

"Okay, announce that Flynn is out, Harward is in."

I knew at that second if I didn't say something, I'd become the next National Security Advisor. And in my gut, I did not want them to make that decision for me. I wanted to make that decision.

"Mr. President, thank you, that's wonderful," I said. "I am honored and humbled, but let's just hold on a few moments on that."

"What?"

It was obvious that the President did not expect this reaction.

"You don't want to be the National Security Advisor?" he said.

I smiled and shook my head in the affirmative.

"I think I do," I said. "But I need to think about it first. You just threw this on me. Can you give me a day, forty-eight hours?"

Trump politely accepted my explanation.

"You've got forty-eight hours."

Everyone got up as the President left and then I beat feet to the airport and a plane to Orlando. I was sitting at the bar in the United Airlines lounge having a snack, when my picture popped up on the large TV screen announcing my appointment to be National Security Advisor. The guy next to me in the lounge, whom I hadn't talked to, looked over at me.

"Isn't that you?"

I looked up at the screen again.

"Looks like me," I said.

I got up and went to my gate, feeling the pressure. I didn't accept the job, but no doubt my bosses in Orlando were going to have questions. Two people called me before I boarded the airplane.

"Congratulations, you've been selected for one of the most powerful positions in the world," they said.

What the hell are they talking about? I thought.

I knew what the job entailed: twenty-four-hour days, seven days a week, which I knew I could handle but the timing just wasn't right. I landed in Orlando and went straight to the conference and pulled my bosses aside.

"I've got to deal with this," I said. "I need some time off, so I'll be in my room if you need me."

At that point, I was just struggling to keep up with everything. Once I got into my room, I started making calls, talking to everyone, and apparently, a lot of people wanted to talk to me.

General Jim Mattis.

Dennis McDonough, former National Security Advisor for President Obama.

Admiral Michael Mullens, former Chairman of the Joint Chiefs of Staff (my Battalion Officer while I was a student at the Naval Academy).

Admiral Jim Stavridis, former NATO Supreme Allied Commander (the Midshipman Brigade Commander while I was a student at the Naval Academy).

I talked to anyone I knew who could give me advice. Mattis wanted me on the team. He, and almost everyone else I talked to, thought I was the right guy and could help guide the right foreign policy. And I thought I had the skillset for that.

After all the advice, I made the most important call home. I'd already made my wife aware of the offer, but we hadn't had a chance to discuss it. My wife was adamantly opposed to me taking the job.

"Bob, you've done this for forty years," she said.

She had a point.

I had spent forty years doing whatever the country told me to do. I wasn't sure I wanted to put on a suit and tie every day at 5:30 a.m. again, work until 11:00 p.m., and take calls all night, seven days a week, for what could be another four years. And then there was the financial aspect. I'd gotten out of the military and was making some money that would have a long-term impact on my wife, my two daughters, and my grandchildren. After all I put them through, they sure deserved it.

"We'll support you if you want to do that," my wife said at the end of our call. "But, is that what you want to do?"

This balance between the job, what we're accomplishing, and the sense of family and community, is critical for any team. And when I served at the National Security Council from 2003 to 2005, that's what I felt we had. It was the best and brightest from the State Department, CIA, Departments of Defense and Treasury, and others. It really was a cohesive team that mutually supported and looked after each other. That was from the top down and the bottom up and that's because I know President Bush demanded it. His teams embraced it. I didn't have a sense of how this team was functioning at the White House. That made me question how effective we could be in foreign policy and meeting the President's objectives. I liked the President's policies and his approach to shaking up the status quo of Washington bureaucracy. I believe this is why he is so popular with the American people. They want someone to fight on their behalf against big, intrusive, self-serving government.

So, with all of that rattling around in my head, I wrote a letter to President Trump and did something I hadn't ever done. I was the yes guy until this moment, but in my letter, I told the President no, or at least not now: "I know you are in for the long haul, and I want to ensure you understand that I remain on the bench, ready to serve should you need me, and when the time is right for both of us."

I faxed the letter up to Bannon and he acknowledged he got it. And then the next morning I went back to the conference. But not without some regret. I knew I had failed to answer the call of service, I hadn't fought the good fight for the country, the President, or my shipmates.

SAYING NO IS NOT EASY

20 February 2017

President Donald J. Trump
The White House
1600 Pennsylvania Avenue, N.W.
Washington, DC 20500

Mr. President,

I feel obliged to write this letter to you, predicated on the stories surrounding my decision not to accept the offer to serve as your National Security Advisor.

As a Naval Officer, and US Navy SEAL serving in uniform for nearly forty years, I took an oath to faithfully serve and defend this great country of ours. While I clearly understood and accepted my obligation, it took me a full career to understand the sacrifices that came with it. It included recurring deployments, constantly moving, and making performance of my duties, a priority in my life. Ironic, in that while I was a son of a career Naval Officer, I still did not clearly understand the full scope of the commitment, or sacrifice, that my father made, until I experienced it.

While I deployed often, and served overseas, my career, for even a SEAL, was unusual. On six different occasions during my career, I was called in the middle of the night for no-notice deployments (on 9-11 it was the middle of the day), where everything else in my life (family, friends, and commitments) were put on hold or disregarded, to immediately depart and go in harm's way, to address our nation's most pressing National Security needs. Each of these periods cover 6 to 8 months of my life, and in one case, two years. I had no options or choices, as this was part of my obligation which I readily accepted, and for which I was educated and trained to perform. I also knew I was the right person for these situations.

Your offer was another similar call to duty on very short notice requiring me to put everything else in my life on hold, but I also knew I was the right man for the position. More importantly, I also saw this as a commitment, similar to my military deployments, that required 24 hours a day, 7 days a week for the next 4 years. The exception in this case, and the extraordinary dilemma for me, was that for the first time, I had a choice – a very difficult one.

Unfortunately, the timing for your offer of the NSA was not right for me, or my family, based on several factors.

Just to set the record straight;

- I was incredibly impressed by the collective team we met with, to include the Vice President, Secretary Mattis, Jared, Steve, and Rince. It would have been an honor and pleasure to serve with them.
- They were fully accommodating of all of my prerequisites, willing to allow me to pick my team, and supported the processes and procedures I thought necessary to accomplish the mission.
- I have, and had no doubts, on how we would address your National Security concerns to meet all of your objectives.

I know you are in for the long haul, and I want to ensure you understand, that I remain on the bench, ready to serve should you need me, and when the time is right for both of us.

With utmost respect,

Robert S. Harward

Robert S. Harward, Vice Admiral USN (ret) SEAL
Chief Executive Lockheed Martin UAE

Many people ask me if I regret not taking the job. I had always believed that guilt and regret are useless, if not damaging, emotions. These emotions and thoughts should only be applied to deciding what you should do but torturing yourself over it after the decision is just a self-inflicted wound. After the fact, they do nothing for you but make you suffer. Move on. At the end of the day, you've got to trust yourself and believe in yourself, even sometimes when it doesn't align with others. As my dad taught me, I was responsible and accountable for myself. Others have an impact, others will advise me, but at the end of the day, you own it, and you live with that.

By saying no, in this case—and don't forget, this was uncharted water for me because never in my life had I ever said no—I realized no gave me more options, more choices, and more opportunities than saying yes. Regardless, I remain on the bench ready to serve.

My decision opened the door for a lot of other amazing opportunities.

I chose another course. I built financial security for my family. I jumped onto Mt. Everest. Motorcycled across Mongolia. I'm spending time with my family. I'm on the speaking circuit. It opened a whole range of wonderful adventures. The only time in my life I've really said no, and it worked out damn well. I was never politically aligned for any of the jobs I got. Nor did I aspire or come up with a master plan. I just said yes. While saying no felt foreign, it just opened another path. No became another yes, in a way. It was another lane to pursue something.

Look forward. I always do.

CHAPTER 9

Your Most Important Bank Account Is Yourself

It's not every day you get asked to break a world record over a plate of penne pasta.

It started on a morning in October 2019. I got a call from an officer I served with at SEAL Team THREE.

"Hey, do you remember Freddy Williams?" he asked me.

I did.

"Freddy ran air ops."

"Well, I heard he's in UAE," the SEAL officer said.

I lived in Abu Dhabi and oversaw Middle East business for a large US defense contractor. Turned out Freddy was in the United Arab Emirates doing business. He ran Complete Parachute Solutions, which built high-altitude parachute equipment and training for the military. I wasn't sure why he was in my neck of the woods, but when I got off the phone, I called Freddy. We caught up and Freddy asked me if I was available to meet that night.

"Let's have dinner," he said.

We met at the hotel Freddy was staying at in Abu Dhabi and we ate at the restaurant on the bottom floor. He and I talked glory days and caught up on team gossip. We also talked a little bit about our respective businesses. We were just getting our main course when Freddy asked me if I was still jumping.

"Oh, yeah, I kept my professional rating," I said. "I'm up to about three-thousand jumps."

I did a lot of charity jumps, I even parachuted into President Trump's home at Mar-a-Lago for an event. Flying through the air at 130 miles per hour, maneuvering like a bird never gets boring and always gets the adrenaline flowing no matter how many times I do it. Similar to sex in that it always just seems to get better.

Freddy smiled.

"Do you want to go on an adventure with us?"

That question is like catnip to me. Was there any doubt about what I was going to say? My mindset is always all the reasons why and none of the reasons why not. I didn't hesitate to say yes.

"Sure," I said without even asking what kind of adventure we were talking about.

"Aren't you going to ask what we're doing?"

I figured it was a jump but wasn't sure where or when. To be honest, I didn't really care.

"We're going to jump on to Mount Everest and set the world record for the highest parachute landing ever," Freddy said.

I couldn't conceal my smile.

"No shit?" I said, truly surprised.

No one in the world jumps on top of the world's highest mountains. Jumpers don't land at over 20,000 feet in a parachute.

You're lucky if you land at 4,000 feet, or if you're in Colorado, you might land on something like 6,000 feet, but no one is jumping out of helicopters at 26,000 feet and landing at 23,000 feet. It was exactly the kind of challenge I lived for and couldn't wait to hear how Freddy planned to pull it off, no doubt using one of his state-of-the-art rigs. The only hang-up was the timeline.

"We leave tomorrow," Freddy said. "Can you make it?"

I took a beat to check the schedule on my phone. I had meetings, of course, but I could reschedule all of them with a few emails or phone calls. Nothing was going to keep me out of the parachute harness.

"I can do that."

I left dinner and returned to my house and packed my gear. I canceled my upcoming meetings for the next couple of weeks and made sure my business was on autopilot while I was gone. My last call was to my wife and daughters in the United States. With the time difference, they were just starting their day. After the normal small talk and catching up with everyone, I hit them with the news.

"I'm going to go to Everest," I told them. "We're going to jump on Everest and try to set this world record."

There was a pause on the line. I knew they were trying to process what I'd told them. Throughout our lives I had thrown shocks at them on a recurring basis. The notice that we were moving to another country in a matter of days, that they were being evacuated from a country that night, that I was leaving for war in a few hours, and much more. They didn't see any of them coming, and this one continued that trend. Thank goodness, this did not require them to do anything.

I knew my wife. If she was being honest, she probably anticipated this type of call. Maybe not the specifics, but the sentiment. My daughter, who grew up with a SEAL father and was married to a SEAL, knew the mindset but still couldn't help but inject some logic into the conversation.

"Grandpas don't do this sort of thing."

I laughed but added, "I'm in great shape, and this will be a great adventure."

We took a commercial flight from Dubai to Kathmandu, Nepal. This was my first chance to meet the other seventeen men on the expedition. There were a dozen jumpers in all, including former special forces soldiers and airmen who had become professional skydivers with tens of thousands of jumps. These were very serious, experienced, professional parachutists who made a career out of it. But it was clear that none of them focused on physical training like I did.

We could see Everest as we landed. I'd never been on the mountain. I'd flown around it, but I never climbed it. But if this went well, I was excited to get on the mountain.

We recovered our gear and boarded a small, twin-engine turboprop that makes frequent daylight flights between Lukla and Kathmandu. Lukla is a small town in northeast Nepal. Situated at 9,380 feet, it is a popular place for visitors to the Himalayas near Mount Everest to arrive. It is referred to as the city with no wheels because the terrain is so steep and all means of transportation from that point on were purely legs-based (two or four).

Lukla is served by the Tenzing-Hillary Airport, which has a single, very short and steep airstrip. High winds, cloud cover, and changing visibility make the approach dicey, and often mean flights get delayed or the airport closes. There are no night flights to Lukla.

As we approached, I noticed the runway was short. The designers compensated for it by how steep it was. It's at a fifteen- or twenty-degree angle, so the plane lands going toward the mountain. It touches down at the low point of the runway and the plane's momentum takes it straight up the hill so the plane stops before running into the town. When you fly out of Lukla, the plane starts at the top of the hill and it runs down and looks like it falls off the runway and then finally catches air and starts climbing out of the valley.

I don't think my adrenaline waned until after we got our gear and headed into town. Lukla was bustling with kids, livestock, and local shops catering to climbers and trekkers heading to Everest. The streets smelled of cardamom, cinnamon, and cumin. It was a beautiful clear day with Carolina blue skies and fat, marshmallow-like clouds. It was a relatively warm day and our team of eighteen was full of excitement and anticipation of the adventure that awaited us. Everyone had an energetic bounce in their step as we worked our way into a nearby valley. Our objective for the first night was in the immediate valley below Lukla, where we would start our ascent. We got to the guesthouse and everyone crashed for the night.

The next morning, we started to climb. We went from 9,000 to 12,000 feet in an effort to climatize. When we got to 12,000, a helicopter met us there with our gear. Before we could make the final ascent, we had to test the equipment first through a series of jumps. We jumped at 12,000 and then we hiked up to 14,000 feet and jumped there for a day or two, then to 16,000 feet,

18,000 feet, and ultimately our final base camp at over 20,000 feet. Our final jumps were at the base of Ama Dablam, another famous peak near Everest. Living conditions at the final base camp at Ama Dablam consisted of a series of one-man tents with a team tent used for planning and meals.

The test jumps weren't easy. We carried a rucksack with climbing gear (in case you missed the landing zone) oxygen tanks (to compensate for the altitude) and the landing zones were very small. If you missed, and hopefully were not injured, you were climbing out of the steep rock- and bolder-covered mountains. They tested more than just the gear. Freddy was also testing the team to see who could overcome the rigors of the environment to complete the mission.

There were only four slots on the actual record setting jump but a dozen jumpers competed to do it. Everyone was affected differently by the altitude, as most of us had never lived at 21,000 feet for a week. That's the rub. Acclimation was the key to survival.

I noticed in the two weeks of hiking and climbing, many of these guys weren't in good shape. They were sucking air. In fact, some of them were experiencing altitude problems like headaches and nausea. Some of the symptoms were so severe that the guys had trouble getting out of bed. I felt the altitude, but my symptoms were mild and didn't last past a couple of days. Between jumps, I still worked out. I pushed myself running hills and doing bodyweight exercises. I kept investing in my body with the understanding that if you smoked or drank or were overweight, it would detract from your ability to assimilate and function at altitude.

And a day without exercise is wasted in my mind. In my former profession, they gave me two hours a day to work out, and I've always maintained that. I still do two hours of strenuous exercise a day, like clockwork, as hard as I can go. I love the physical adrenaline rush. I love how good it makes me feel. I love competition, so I leveraged that into a career. Every day, I also check my weight. I check my resting pulse, and I check my blood pressure. I keep honing my instrument so that when I need it, it responds.

Shit breaks.

I've been shot, I've been stabbed, I have been knocked out on recurring occasions. They found a hole in my heart. I've detached biceps. I've torn Achilles. But I'm sixty-seven and I'm still physically smoking most of the SEALs I know.

I treat my body like the most important asset and investment I have, and I religiously take care of it. I invest all I can into it, planning for a lifetime of dividends. Unlike social security, I know it will be there when I need it and it is much more essential than your smartphone. Investing in yourself is the most important bank account you have.

After two weeks, we made our final test jump at 21,000 feet. A tough landing zone because it was located at the bottom of a large crater on the side of the mountain. There was no alternative place to land. Once you entered the crater, you had to astutely and vigorously work your parachute to avoid the walls in order to land on the designated spot. There were no other options. You either hit the spot or crashed into the side of the mountain. It had a high pucker factor.

Freddy and I jumped together. I had a clean opening and deftly piloted the chute into the crater, landing upright within a few feet and seconds of Freddy. Two teammates enjoying the success of a high-risk adventure, not dissimilar to our times in the team, with the exception that no one was shooting at us on this mission.

That night, after we secured all our gear and had dinner, we mustered in the tent for the final selection meeting. I'd had a good series of jumps and was confident I was in the mix to go. But you're never sure until you hear your name. It was one of those "damned if you do, damned if you don't" moments, in which everyone wished the best for all, but also everyone wanted the opportunity to jump at the top of the world. It was uncomfortably quiet.

"OK, we selected four people to go," Freddy said.

As he started to name the final four, I heard my name but not Freddy's. I was buzzing, but I wanted to know why he wasn't going. He was my teammate, the leader of the expedition, and the whole reason I was on this great adventure. After the meeting, I pulled Freddy aside.

"Why me?" I said.

"Because you're in good shape," he said. "We know you won't have problems at that altitude. You're working out up here while these other guys are just trying to get some rest and sleep."

I was humbled and somewhat embarrassed. How could I go without him? He was the only reason I was there.

"Thanks," I said. "But why aren't you going?"

"I'm leading the overall effort," he said. "I need to run it, not do it, you know?"

Mission first, people always. He took care of his men and made sure we were ready but also knew our best chance of success was with him on the wheel to make sure everything went smoothly. Freddy was a leader first, and always.

A couple of days later, we were ready to make the attempt from our base camp in Ama Dablam at 21,000 feet. Sherpas took wind ratings as we milled around the helipad, waiting for the green light. It was a crystal-clear day but brisk. I didn't feel the temperature. My adrenaline was pumping and I couldn't sit still.

Freddy came out of the command tent and waved us over.

"The winds are picking up," Freddy said. "Go back to your tents."

I went back to my tent and started checking my gear. After about an hour of waiting, I crashed for a nap until yelling woke me.

"It's on! It's on!"

Everyone was running around the camp, getting on their gear. The helicopters cranked up. Freddy met me on my way to the helipad and gave me a thumbs-up.

"OK, you're good," he said.

We were using two helicopters. I was the second jumper. Kevin went first. His bird left first and disappeared into the clouds. My helicopter took off next and followed it. The helicopters were stripped out of any excess weight. It was just me and a pilot, but it was still struggling to make altitude. I prayed we could get up to altitude and jump out without the helicopter crashing, and from what I was assessing, the odds were about even.

You know, my girls were probably right. Grandpas don't do this kind of shit.

At this point, there was no backing out. Over the radio I heard Freddy report that Kevin had jumped successfully. I was sitting in the open door. The curvature of the earth was on the horizon. Mountains stretched for hundreds of miles in any direction covered in crystal clear snow. The wind was howling. I was looking at Mount Everest in the eye. The drop zone looked like a snow-covered church steeple.

I stepped out on the skid and verified everything was clear heading to the drop zone. The pilot was watching me. I gave him a thumbs-up. He returned it and I stepped off the skid.

"*Adios, amigo*—I'm out of here."

Usually when you jump from a plane, you transition from the plane's forward speed to gravity pulling you down. But the helicopter was barely moving forward, and the wind was so high—70 knots—that it felt like I was going backward.

To my right, I watched the helicopter dive down. It was flying faster than I was falling. It felt like being in a vacuum. It was just a straight drop. I fought to stay level and keep from spinning because as soon as I transitioned to gravity, I had to throw my parachute. The wind battered me as I felt gravity take hold. I threw my parachute and felt the tug of the lines as it deployed. For a second, I relaxed.

"I've got canopy. I'm good to go. Oh, fuck! No, I'm not good to go—that wind."

The wind blew me off course to the right. I pulled hard on the right handle and lined up the drop zone again. My heart was pumping adrenaline like a fast-moving river as I wrestled with the parachute controls to set up my approach. The drop zone looked incredibly small. Miss it and there was a good chance I would die.

The whole jump was a physics experiment performed at 100 miles an hour. How close can I fly up to Everest before my turn because I have to run with the winds and still stay in the drop zone? If I hit the mountain, or miss the landing zone, it's a long and dangerous hike out, as long as you're not injured. Any serious injury was fatal.

I tugged on the riser handles until I lined up the landing when a gust sped me up. I tried to correct my course. I was going to miss the drop zone when I felt a flare of wind and then the snow under my boots. I was cruising at 30 knots and the flare took a little off the forward speed.

I sank into three feet of snow. It felt like a soft pillow but served as the perfect buffering mechanism. I took a few deep breaths before the altitude hit me like a baseball bat. I was still at 23,000 feet. Every step as I climbed out of the snow and gathered my gear felt like I was carrying five hundred pounds, not just a parachute and associated gear.

I was out of adrenaline and crashing. It was a real burden to just breathe and walk, and yet I still had to pick up my parachute and walk back up to the rendezvous in waist-high snow so the helicopter could come in and pick me up.

It was a struggle, but I slowly gathered up my chute and gear and trudged over to the landing zone where the helicopters were coming to take us down. Luckily, two Sherpas were stationed on the summit. They stowed my parachute as I climbed into the helicopter. As we descended, the realization that I did something that only a handful of people in the world had ever done hit me and a smile crept across my face. Back at base camp, we were treated to a hero's welcome. But I didn't care about the record. That's not why I did it. It was just the opportunity.

Every aspect of the adventure was just an amazing, incredible experience. I was in a no-lose situation. I got to go to Mount

Everest. I got to hike up to 21,000 feet. I got to live at 21,000 and parachute along the way. It was just another one of the miracles of the life I'd had and the experiences I'd had, all enabled by the Gouge.

It started with the investment in my health. Doing the work every day set me up to jump. It was enabled by my teammate who shared the same career, values, and philosophy that taking care of each other, was equally as important, if not more so. When the time came to climb out on the helicopter skid, I stepped off because of the trust and belief in myself, and that's half of what working out and taking care of yourself does. It gives you that trust and belief in yourself.

No one loves you more than you. Do all of the things that come with that: take care of yourself, invest in yourself, take the adventures, don't hesitate, and don't overthink it.

CHAPTER 10

Community Matters

The prison's walls were over thirty feet high and eight feet deep.

It was impossible to see inside from the outside. There was no gate. Access to the prison was through a three-foot-wide tunnel in the wall. It didn't take much to guard a tunnel opening. That was their security, and like so many things in Afghanistan, it was simple, cheap, and effective.

The warden of the prison in Nimruz, Afghanistan, went into the tunnel first, followed by his staff. When it was my turn, I glanced at my protection detail—a half dozen heavily armed American soldiers in full body armor—and every man shook his head. The tunnel wasn't secure. Going into an Afghan prison with no secondary egress contradicted all security training. No one wanted to crawl through the dirt except for me. I shrugged and followed the warden on my hands and knees into the tunnel.

Unlike my protection detail, I wasn't wearing body armor, nor did I have a long gun, just a pistol tucked into the small of my back. We crawled through the tunnel and emerged into a massive courtyard with hundreds of prisoners milling about, dressed in long shirts and baggy pants of the region. People were talking and cooking, and while I knew I was in a prison, it seemed like a relatively peaceful environment.

The warden—a slight man with a beard of more salt than pepper—led me into the crowd as we toured the facility. He was highlighting to me through his staff the living conditions, what people were in the prison for, and how they handled food. The group of prisoners parted as we walked. Everyone stopped and watched us as we toured. We were probably the most exciting thing they'd seen in a while. A break in the monotony of prison life.

In my peripheral vision, I spotted my security on top of the wall. While I crawled in, they raced to the top of the wall to set up overwatch positions. I got to the far end of the compound with the warden when I heard my protection detail in my earpiece.

"Get the hell out of there."

I paused.

"Why?"

"You're surrounded by about two hundred prisoners, and we can't do shit if they go at you."

I turned to look back and saw what looked like every prisoner in a group behind us. They'd gathered and started to follow us. From above, it looked like I was about to be mobbed. There were too many targets for my security detail. The tension was audible in their voice. From the top of the wall, it looked dire. It was just me and Command Master Chief Bobby Edwards with the warden. I had a Sig Sauer P226 9mm pistol on me with a fifteen-round magazine, which wouldn't keep us alive for long.

But I wasn't worried because on the ground the scene was different.

All around me the prisoners were gathering to shake my hand or just watch me as I toured with the warden. They had smiles and friendly eyes. I could understand some of them—those who spoke Dari—and they weren't angry. They were curious. The prisoners had only seen Americans from afar or dressed in body armor and helmets. I looked human in just a shirt and fatigue pants. We were something new. The warden introduced me and I spoke to them in Farsi.

Minds blown.

I wasn't just an American uniform anymore. I spoke their language. I knew their culture. But I was also treating them with some humanity. A lot of the men in the courtyard were economic prisoners. They couldn't pay bills or owed money. Very few were in there for violent crimes. These men were the poorest of the poor in Afghanistan. The discarded of Afghan society but still part of the human community.

If the Gouge is a contract with humanity, then that contract extends to every community. Living the Gouge meant finding common ground with all races, creeds, sexes, and classes. And because I lived that way, I was the perfect person to come to Afghanistan and rebuild the civil infrastructure as a 3-Star Vice Admiral. I got the job reforming the prison system after General Dave Petraeus took command of NATO forces in Afghanistan in 2010.

"The Taliban are not the only enemy of the people," he wrote in a twenty-four-point memo outlining his strategy. "The people are also threatened by inadequate governance, corruption, and abuse of power—recruiters for the Taliban."

Petraeus wanted to rebuild the country's social, financial, and justice systems because the Taliban often gained ground just by providing governance. He and McChrystal came up with the idea to launch a task force around the rule of law and detention operations. Not only our detention of enemy combatants but all the prisons in Afghanistan to ensure training of the guards, case management systems, and due process. We were going to build courthouses and train lawyers and judges.

Hence my visit to the prison in Nimruz and all of the twenty-six provinces. I got to spend time in every prison, talking to judges, building court houses, roads, and providing medical care. It was nation-building. But it wasn't that expensive, and I believed it had greater impact than the other missions, such as building wells, irrigation systems, or schools.

My colleagues laughed when they found out about my new job. "Who'd you piss off? That's a career-ender." But I didn't see it that way. I looked at it as a great adventure. It got me back to Afghanistan—a country I loved—and not as a man hunter. I was building a community instead of tearing it down.

My perception of the country was informed by hitchhiking there as a teenager in the early seventies. I liked the Afghan people. I understood the culture. The Afghan people were hospitable, humble, and wanted education. But they also lived in abject poverty, struggling to survive every day, for weeks, months, years, and decades. This is the common denominator for every Afghan. In the seventies, it wasn't much different, except it was a peaceful nation. No war, no hostilities, and a safe place to travel—especially for Westerners.

It seemed like the perfect counterbalance to my early assignments. We accomplished our mission of getting rid of al Qaeda and those that attacked us on 9-11 by March 2002, but instead of brokering a peace deal and leaving as victors, we kept bringing in more and more troops.

I just didn't understand how that was going to sit with the local Afghans because we brought them in for more war fighting instead of nation-building. My new assignment allowed me to lean into the Gouge and really go everywhere in Afghanistan and show the best side of American military power. My task force wasn't interested in war. We were interested in getting through the war, building the nation and making every Afghan person a contributor to that growth. Most importantly, building trust in a government that had their well-being in mind and purpose.

From the first day in Kabul, I beat this theme into every member of the task force, which is why there was no way I wasn't going into that prison.

"Look, guys, here's our mission, here's what we're going to do. We're going to share all our skills, so yeah, we're going to try to make all these Afghans smarter and better than they were when they came into this system. We're going to share knowledge; we're going to make them smarter than their village."

Everyone in the task force embraced that concept. We all believed that we had a big, if not a bigger, impact than the war fighting. Not just by what we did in the prisons but how we approached people, and how we worked with them. What they saw of Americans and what we were committed to.

Our unit coin was a round circle with the peace sign. It was also a great bottle opener. The peace sign was iconic and reflective of the time when I first came to Afghanistan in 1972. That's what we were after. We were trying to build Afghanistan in a model of peace, community, and education. Not dissimilar to the Afghanistan I had experienced in the 1970s, or at least the peaceful part.

My first stop once I took command was a visit with Hamid Karzai, the president of Afghanistan. I'd helped bring Karzai into the country in the early days of the war and knew him well. Karzai embraced our purpose and goal because he knew we had to find a political solution and this program contributed to that. The Afghans wanted to build their country. They were tired of war and the way to really influence not only the Afghans but also the Taliban is to show compassion in building their country.

One of my generals told me I had to work with Ashraf Ghani, who was serving as the finance minister and would later go on to be president right up until the 2021 fall. He was a Western-educated intellectual whose family and tribe were powerful, respected, and influential. I spent the first part of our meeting explaining the mission and intent. When I was done, he started laughing. I was confused.

"My family used to kidnap people and hold them till they capitulated to our demands or paid some form of compensation," he said. "We used to take prisoners."

I laughed.

"We have a lot in common," I said.

We agreed that the Taliban were just wayward Afghans that could be brought back into the fold. Ghani didn't want to be at war with them. His thought was we needed to unite this country by finding common ground that brings us all together as one nation. I didn't know if it was possible but I remember that's how the Afghanistan I knew before the war existed. There was always this communist angle that played out after the war that divided the country but before that, you didn't have those issues. And building the prison systems, building the support structure, would be a powerful counter-message to the Taliban and one they couldn't deny.

Ghani helped us guide the ministries. So much so that I had a full Afghan team that lived and worked with us. We built the Afghan team to mirror my own team of bureaucrats, lawyers, judges, and civil affairs experts. We were one-on-one doing this together because not only were we doing it in the civilian world, but we were also doing it in the Afghan military. We built living quarters for them and trained their guards; their guards stood watching with us. The whole system was built to work us out of a job.

Some of the most exciting stuff was in the prisons. Not only did we create a working case management system, but we also made the facility more efficient. We brought in toilets that use bacteria to eat the feces so it's still a big pit but that pit never needs to be dug up because the bacteria you put inside eats it. We brought those into the prisons to enhance the sanitary conditions. We built gardens and taught drip irrigation so the prisoners could grow their own food. We built industrial-sized kitchens so the prisoners could cook and enhance the quality and quantity of the food for the prison population, a common concern across all the prisons in Afghanistan.

Every one of our actions was rooted in the Gouge. We were taking care of the men to our left and right. We were building a community by sharing best practices. Our purpose was to improve the Afghan justice system and we were leaning into that purpose.

I left Nimruz with so many ideas. If we were going to empower the Afghans to create a better country, we had to start at the bottom. Prisoners learned how to garden, make pottery, anything so that when they were released, they had a skill that contributed to their community.

That was the end stage.

The prisoners, when they came out, had skill sets directly applicable to their villages. We were sharing the Gouge and the thoughts and resources to help improve each of these prisons and earn their respect, not only of the wardens and guards but of all the prisoners.

Leading the task force was more satisfying than the jobs I had hunting guys down and fighting them. I felt I had a bigger impact on the country and the people of Afghanistan. In my opinion, this was the true path to changing and helping countries like Afghanistan adapt, grow, and prosper. I won't say democracy was the goal. More so, trust and confidence in a government that would address the needs of the people.

That's what I hoped for in Afghanistan. Unfortunately, that is not what happened, and I am afraid that Afghanistan will return to the desperately poor country it has always been, but now governed by a repressive and harsh government more interested in what the people can do for them than what they can do for the people—at the same time, perverting the values of Islam.

Leading Rule of Law, Afghan Prisons and US Detention Operations from 2010 to 2012, where we instigated a case management system, built out health care, provided court houses, trained judges, and a plethora of other nation-building efforts that directly supported the Afghan people was one of the most rewarding jobs of my career.

CHAPTER 11

Great Leaders Share Gouge

I was blessed the last two decades to have served with leaders who understood the Gouge, even if they didn't know the term. We never discussed it and I'd never written it down, but they were aligned to the Gouge philosophy. They treated people as important, if not more so, than the mission. And because of that, they and the collective team achieved beyond expectations.

Gouge leaders all have the same qualities. Being a Gouge leader is putting your people and team first and foremost to meet the mission, empowering them and supporting them to do their job. The best leaders are rarely the smartest people in the room; instead, they ask the best questions. Each one has emotional intelligence. They understand people and how to build authentic rapport. They can harness the best of people by leading by example and then inspiring them to follow.

A few of the best Gouge leaders I served with were President George W. Bush, Condoleezza Rice, Steve Hadley, Fran Townsend, General David Petraeus, General Stan McChrystal, General

Wayne Downing, Admiral Tim Keating, Admiral Tom Fargo, and Admiral Bill McRaven.

Bill and I spent twenty years flipping jobs with each other, so it made sense we'd install or inherit the same kind of culture. Plus, we came from the same service. We understood how a team was the be-all and end-all and the importance of working as one to survive and prosper.

But few leaders embodied the Gouge more than Marine Corps General Jim Mattis. He operated at a completely different level. Mattis focused on people with passion and purpose. He was the kind of guy who could stop and talk to people and the person would walk away thinking he was Mattis' best friend, and not because he got played but because at that moment Mattis was his best friend.

One of the best examples of Mattis acting as a Gouge leader was one Christmas when he was commanding US Central Command in Tampa, Florida. Mattis was a bachelor, and he came to work on Christmas Day to get some work done. But when he got to the headquarters building, he found a young airman on desk duty. Mattis asked if he had a family, and the young airman responded yes. Mattis was single and his mother and brothers were all in Washington state. He wasn't required to be tree-side to open gifts or at the holiday dinner table. But the airman was missing out on his children's Christmas celebration.

Mattis sent him home.

"I'll take the watch for you," he said. "I've got nowhere I need to be."

The airman was stunned and then grateful. At no point did he expect Mattis—the commanding general of all American forces in the Middle East—to man the front desk of his own headquarters during a holiday.

Who does that kind of stuff? Only someone who believes people are just as important—even more important—than the mission. That airman went home to his family feeling important. He knew his commander cared about his well-being and in doing so, he reaffirmed their purpose to take care of one another and complete the mission.

I was lucky to serve under him at Joint Forces Command. I was promoted from rear admiral (one star) to vice admiral (three stars) in order to take the job. I skipped rear admiral upper half (two stars) and was a little nervous in my new position. It was our first command meeting and Mattis introduced me as Vice Admiral Bob Harward. It sounded funny coming out of his mouth, and I think it showed in my body language. I was tense, so Mattis did what he did best—read the room and let out some of the pressure.

"He's a young buck," Mattis said. "A rate-grabber for jumping from one to three stars."

That got a laugh, since I knew everyone was thinking it too. But that was the only laugh because Mattis had a bigger message and delivered it with conviction.

"Make no mistake about it—he's not my deputy," Mattis said. "He is my co-commander. When he speaks, I'm speaking. We speak with one voice."

The words empowered me in the eyes of the staff, but they did more for me. It theoretically put the responsibility of command on my shoulders. I wasn't only a senior staffer there to support Mattis. I was there to help him lead and in doing so take responsibility for my actions. Mattis knew those words would ignite my purpose to serve and align my efforts with his because we both had skin in the game. I left that meeting more committed than when I went in because I no longer had time to worry about my promotion. I had a command to help lead.

How can you not trust and believe in a guy like that? It wasn't just me. He had the same faith in everyone in his command.

I consider Mattis—Jim to me—my swim buddy, meaning that we look after each other and take care of each other, which has been our relationship for the last twenty years. In my opinion, Jim is the most humble and unassuming leader that I have known in my career. No one can hold a candle to him. Like my father, Jim has always had an unblinding faith in me. He helped me to reach my potential and did everything he could to promote that growth while still holding me accountable along the way. Jim did the same for many people, which is why he is such a beloved leader. In essence, Jim lives the Gouge and he often used it in ways that I had never seen before. I aspire to do the same.

I do not think that Jim's decision to resign as Secretary of Defense under Trump was a shotgun decision, nor was it much of a surprise to me. We spoke often and I observed several times when he and the President moved in different directions on policy that Jim felt strongly about. Transgenders in the military, Space Command, and a military Parade in Washington, DC are all issues that any Secretary of Defense would have strong opinions on, but Forward Presence and Engagements have always been a bedrock of US foreign policy, and a cornerstone of our military capabilities. In my opinion, Forward Presence and Military Power Projection have been the determining enablers that have defined the world order for the past eight decades.

I believe pulling out of Syria was a decision and policy position that ran counter to what Jim Mattis believed in. Since the end of World War II, when we didn't bring all the troops home (like my father), we built and maintained a forward presence in Europe and Asia that we have supported for over eight decades, with great success. A powerful testament to consistent policies that were politically supportable. This forward presence allowed us to influence and support the growth of like-minded governments who aspired to mature in line with the values, processes, and the prosperity that we have. As President Bush said in his last meetings with SEALs during his administration, "My father fought an ideological and radical enemy who is now one of our closest allies and an economic powerhouse – Japan". In his opinion, a dedicated forward presence of a strong US military was the enabler that made this evolution possible. I believe the same strategy and policies in the Middle East could have been just as productive, understanding that it would take decades to mature.

Being a follower of the Gouge, purpose is the foundation and when that goes, it is over. And for Mattis, there was no reason to stay. Case in point, when Mattis left CENTCOM and retired, he drove himself back to his hometown of Walla Walla, Washington, stopping on the way to visit with Gold Star families. It was important to him to show his gratitude and respect for the people who had lost their family members in war. In his mind, these families sacrificed everything for their country and the mission. By stopping to visit them, Mattis was putting people first because they'd given their lives for the mission.

It was the Gouge personified.

Another master of the Gouge was President George W. Bush. Every national politician—agree with them or not—has charisma. They're master communicators. President Bush came on the scene as a plain-spoken Texan. He was the guy who people wanted to have a beer with, which was ironic because Bush was sober. Sometimes that is an act to build rapport with voters, but Bush really was down-to-earth, humble, and accommodating. It surprised me because he was the son of a president and lived a life of privilege.

I worked in the Bush White House from June 2003 to April 2005 as a member of the National Security Council staff. During my tenure, he was kind enough to let me bring my daughter Maggie into the White House to meet with him. My daughter was a senior at San Diego State and we met the president in the Oval Office. Neither of us had ever thought we would find ourselves in that position. I was just a guy on the national security staff. It wasn't like I had any real power.

But as soon as we entered the Oval Office, we had the president's full attention. He had a full day—most presidents have very little downtime—but he took a real interest in my daughter, including remembering she was in college.

"Maggie, I heard you're at school," Bush said.

"Yes, sir," she said. "I'm at San Diego State."

He laughed.

"Well, isn't that the number one party school in the country?" Bush asked, a sly smile on his lips. "Do you even go to class?"

My daughter was a fair student studying criminal justice. I knew she was going to class but being my daughter, she wasn't going to pass up a chance to give it back, even to the leader of the free world.

"Only when it's cloudy," Maggie quickly retorted.

Bush turned to me.

"Bob," he said through a chuckle, "our daughters have a lot in common."

I left that meeting elated. It was invigorating to have someone like Bush take a few minutes to connect with me and my daughter. From that moment on, I had complete trust and confidence in him. I'd do anything he wanted because he made me and my family as important as anything he was doing that day. That's what the Gouge is all about. How do you empower, support, and care? Through your actions. By showing your people that you see them not as a way to accomplish a mission but as teammates working with you to accomplish a mission.

Months later, I was called to meet with Bush via video teleconference. He was flying on Air Force One in late 2004 and wanted to test the new system that had just been installed. I was working out in the gym of an undisclosed underground facility when one of his communications staff came in to get me. They wanted to test it early and they hustled me to the situation room. I pulled on a coat and tie but left my pants in the locker room as I knew I'd be sitting behind a table and the video teleconference would only show me from the waist up.

I sat down and pulled the mic close. The flat screen went from black to a full-color shot of the president in his office on Air Force One. We made small talk and checked the audio and video feed to make sure both were stable. The test was a success. We were about to sign off when Bush had one more question.

"Hey, Bob," the president said. "Can you stand up?"

I played dumb and tried to sign off.

"No," Bush said. "Don't sign off yet. Can you stand up for me?"

I reluctantly stood up. Bush laid into me for showing up for a meeting with the president without pants. As he put it, I was half naked. A member of the communications staff had dimed me out and Bush couldn't resist giving me shit for it.

To be clear, he didn't care that I was wearing shorts. We completed the mission, but the joke broke down some of the pomp and circumstance around the office. There was no question he was the boss. But humor made him approachable, which meant staffers with important information wouldn't hesitate to share it. It was a genius way of making sure he was getting the best Gouge.

I still talk to President Bush. We recently discussed his new passion—painting.

"Bob, you gotta do this painting thing," he said, going on to tell me about how calm it makes him.

But painting probably wasn't for me.

"Sir, I've never painted," I said.

"Bob, never had I either, but it engages your mind; it brings you peace. You'll be great, Bob."

I'm not sure I'll ever paint. You know me by now. I'm more of the active sort. But the fact that he would be telling me, even persuading me, to do it meant something. His passing this Gouge onto me was indicative of that personal connection, his interest in me, and his belief in people and making sure we had all of the information we need to not only succeed but live our best lives.

What do Mattis and Bush have in common?

They understand how to build a Gouge culture predicated on people first and making sure everyone is armed with the best information so they can not only do the job but so they can sync it with their purpose.

It was an honor for all of us (seven countries of Task Force K-Bar) to receive the Presidential Unit Citation from President George W. Bush. It acknowledged the importance of our partnerships and the impact when we needed it most. These relationships and commitments to our partners are more important than ever before.

I'm in the corporate world now and I see how challenging this is for big companies. Small businesses get this even when they struggle to survive and meet payroll but the big business world has a much different problem. Their value is driven by their shareholders and the return on their investments. I think that's where smaller companies get their innovation—by investing in their people and letting them live up to their purpose and potential. It's why I always loved serving in small teams because it isn't just the mission; it's taking every opportunity to help your team realize their belief, their purpose, and their goals in life. That was the priority and sharing your knowledge and experience with them in all aspects, not just your professional but your personal side, was part of the calculus.

Mattis and Bush spend time doing things for long-term success even though they may not have been the quickest, easiest, or most sexy. I think the same applies to corporate America and I believe most leaders miss it because they care about short-term success, such as their own promotion or stock price and employees see right through that.

The Gouge only works when you share it. Lead by it and live it.

CHAPTER 12

Bum Gouge

If you followed the 2016 US presidential election, I'm sure you are familiar with the name Michael Flynn.

Mike and I served together for many years, and I had a front-row seat to the wild ride he and his family experienced. It was unfortunate because Mike was a senior military officer who had had a very successful career but was lured to the dark side of politics. Many senior military leaders believed he had broken the moral line, meaning that he leveraged his military title and experience to promote political objectives and endorse the Republican candidate, which directly opposed the military apolitical status quo.

I am not as adamant. Once you transition out of uniform, your relevance, beyond your title, is a diminishing asset. Add to that, many other military flag officers had served numerous administrations, with the most infamous National Security Advisor being Brett Scowcroft, who served as the Advisor to Presidents Ford and Bush.

You see, when you step into that political ring, you know that the rules of the game change. It's a different dynamic and one where you leave yourself open to endless probing and scrutiny. Your whole life becomes a feeding frenzy of possible intrigue. Mike's bum Gouge was not fully understanding the new rules of the game. Perhaps he got bad advice. Or maybe he just didn't understand the depth to which his personal life and files would be pillaged. In the end, Mike fell from grace. His honor, integrity, and fidelity were all called into question. And let me tell you, those three virtues are like your virginity. Once they are gone, they are gone forever. However, I know Mike had the best possible intentions and felt he could contribute to the job and administration. He had become a victim of the political landscape.

As you can see from Mike's story, you need to always calibrate yourself to new surroundings or you run the risk of falling prey to bum Gouge. What is true in a combat situation is just as relevant in starting a new job or even a relationship. You must understand what you are getting into and with whom. Mike failed to reset himself when he stepped into a new work environment. He failed to learn the new rules and norms. Best intentions gone astray.

Bum Gouge doesn't just come from making poor choices, though. You can also get bum Gouge from others. It's essential that you look at the source. If you type something into Google these days, you can get ten million results back. That's all Gouge. But not all of it is gonna be good. Hell, most of it is probably bad.

You have to think to yourself: *Is someone trying to sell me something? Does it benefit this person/company in any way if they influence my thinking one way or another? Does this person have credibility?*

You have to be able to flex your critical thinking muscles here if you want to stay ahead of the situation.

Many times, bad Gouge is simply being surrounded by the wrong people. This can be at work or even in your social life. You must have respect and confidence in the people that you are in relationships with. How many times have you heard of business partners who didn't see eye to eye and then ended up taking their whole business down? Same with divorce. Or even taking a job based on someone's recommendation that then didn't pan out so well.

Good Gouge only comes from relationships where everyone is on the same page and working toward the same goal. And this is where character comes into play. The source's experience and intentions are critical and so are their personal attributes. Would you be willing to jump off a bridge because they told you to? Think about this when you are listening to someone's advice or even watching their interactions to learn from them.

Good Gouge and bum Gouge are only differentiated sometimes by experience and the situation you're in.

It's really a thin line and often what starts as bum turns into good after some time. Remember, my father didn't want me to be a SEAL. He was cool with me being an aviator or a ship driver, but he didn't see a bright future as a special warfare operator.

"Goddamnit," he said, exasperated. "I never did think you were this bright; I just didn't think you were this dumb. There's no future in that SEAL stuff."

At the time, that was good Gouge because he was exactly right. There were only two captains—one on each coast—and no admirals. The force was downsizing after the Vietnam War and the Navy found little value in swimming commandos.

But being that I was a stubborn ass, I was willing to risk taking bum Gouge. I didn't care. I wanted to be a SEAL and didn't care if that meant a short naval career. I was going to do it because I knew I'd be good at it and felt a passion for the physical activity.

Thank God I was fortunate. The world changed between when I joined the teams and after September 11, 2001. That good Gouge is now bum Gouge. If you're a midshipman and you want a career in the Navy, the best career to take is a SEAL, if you can make it through BUD/S. If you stay in twenty years, you've got about a 95 percent chance of making captain, and that doesn't exist in any other naval warfare specialty.

Bum gouge may be bad advice or information, but it still helps inform. At the time, in 1983, when my father gave me the advice not to be a SEAL, it was good Gouge. At the time, there were just over a thousand SEALs in all, and only two captains. There wasn't much room for advancement. We had come out of Vietnam and the Navy saw no need for SEALs. My dad was right. But I followed my gut and my passion anyway, and, in time, fortunately, my decision proved right. September 11, 2001, changed everything and made SEALs the force of choice. And I eventually became an admiral. So, in the end, after some time, my dad's good advice became bum Gouge.

As good as Gouge is, as much as it accumulates and grows over time, bad Gouge can do the same in the opposite direction. Bum Gouge can ruin your reputation. It can cost you your job, your marriage, and, in some instances, your life.

Thinking into the future, seeking out bum Gouge and tracking it down to its root is key, especially in leadership positions. Gouge is gouge, you know, so even bum Gouge gives you some information. It lays out a path—even if that choice is not agreeable—and offers a 360-degree look at a choice or problem. Faced with bum Gouge from people you trust, listen and process it. Find its root. Why did the folks in the Trump administration want me to take the job? Experience? Another ally? Proven results? All good but in this case the timing wasn't good, and it wasn't something I personally wanted at the time. Why did my father steer me away from the SEALs? He believed that I would not have a long and fulfilling career as a SEAL, which was an accurate assessment at the time, but in this case, it was something I personally wanted. The Gouge constantly changes as indicated by both of these situations and fate always seems to have an impact.

Learning to discriminate between good and bum Gouge takes time and experience. But it is essential in our information-overloaded society. And sometimes your gut is the deciding vote.

CHAPTER 13

Confrontation Can, and Should Be, Productive

We're a culture of confrontation.

We've always been that way and it is one of the cornerstones in defining our country, for in the end, we have always banded together on the final outcome. Today's confrontations, however, have set a new standard where we're entrenched on opposite sides of a war of ideas and culture. With the deep penetration of social media into every membrane of society, facts and perceptions are incessantly misinterpreted. Just look at COVID. We no longer embrace the same facts or science. Instead, we fight over rumors and bad information. Facebook trolls bombard us with quack science. Anti-vaxxers believe the shot won't protect you against COVID. Instead, it will give you autism or plant a tracking device. I've got news for you: that phone in your pocket is already doing the job.

We've been pulled to the edges, leaving the middle a no-man's-land. Americans are finding refuge on the edges but for all the wrong reasons. This is no way to survive. No society lives long when everyone is at one another's throats and confrontation becomes the coin of the realm to achieve objectives. There is no better time for the Gouge. While it seems like a "shiny, happy people" philosophy, confrontation is part of life and understanding the philosophy and application of the Gouge means you're not always going to agree.

Case in point: it is never a good sign when the commander's office orders you to report to his office. Especially when you were the new guy and shaking up the status quo.

It was October 1986 and after several tours with West Coast SEAL teams, I got a chance to serve with our most elite unit in Virginia Beach. I got to Dam Neck at the end of Richard "Dick" Marcinko's era. A Vietnam veteran and the first commanding officer of SEAL Team SIX, he handpicked members of the unit and it was still very much his good old boys' network when I showed up. The teams were run by the senior enlisted—the Chief Petty Officer mafia—and he trusted them, and they knew it. It allowed them to challenge the leadership of the officers, especially new ones like me.

At the Naval Academy and later in the fleet, there was a clear differentiation between the roles, responsibilities, and most importantly, the accountability of the enlisted force and the officer corps. Those lines became much more nebulous in the SEAL community. Unfortunately, everything about leadership and military order got blurred once you went through the Dam Neck gate.

I'd completed my platoon time in the teams and went through selection and then Green Team. I got to the command

and took over an assault team. But the operators on the team treated every new officer as a temp. For them, this was the final destination, but officers cycled in and out in order to continue their careers. At the end of the day, the team was still the officer's responsibility, and for which they were held accountable. A smart officer leaned on his chiefs but still led them.

At the time, there were only three squadrons and in hindsight I inherited a team with a unique culture. We were known as the "bad boys of blue." It wasn't lost on me that our patch was the skull and crossbones. The other two squadrons were head and shoulders ahead of my guys physically and operationally, which came to a head when we headed west to do some dive training in the Pacific Northwest.

"We're chiefs; we can run this" was their mantra as we planned the trip. I stepped out of the way and let them plan the whole four days of training. It went off the rails right away. We never got a dive in over one hundred feet (nowhere near the standard operational requirement) and ran out of oxygen, used for our diving rebreathing systems, because it was often used as a cure for hangovers.

That was the last straw. I called the team all together.

"OK, boys, put on your fricking G-suits because I'm about to launch you guys to the moon," I said. "You operationally are not meeting the requirements and we would not be able to meet the mission if called upon."

From that point on, I planned the training. We upped our physical fitness training—two hours a day—and spent time in the surf, on the range and in the classroom. After a few training evolutions, I realized my current team wasn't as proficient as the

SEAL team I had come from in San Diego. I had an inflated idea of what it would be like at Dam Neck, but I quickly learned it was a cushy gig. We didn't deploy for six months like the other teams. We traveled around training. We stayed in nice hotels. With all those resources dedicated to one unit, I didn't see the professionalism or the competence that should have been in place with that investment of resources.

It didn't help that there was a lot of drinking. That was one of the traits of the team I inherited at the time. They all drank too much, and I suspected much worse. The culture of the teams didn't align with military values. The only course of action was to change it, but the whole place was made up of alpha males, and if you weren't willing to stand up and fight for your beliefs and what you thought was right, you weren't going to succeed.

I challenged them.

I demanded accountability to one another and the team.

I reminded them they were still in the Navy and not their own entity. We were still a military unit, not a motorcycle gang. We were the force that the country depended on and we had to be more than proficient; we had to be able to conduct the mission when called upon. We could not fail. This was the Gouge for the team. I laid down the gauntlet, and from there it was a daily struggle to see which culture would survive.

You can imagine how popular this made me. Trying to change the culture that had been inculcated since inception. The ability to confront them was all they understood and responded to, but I was never part of the tribe. I was something they had to deal with. After Marcinko and a few others, I was working for the new commanding officer, Captain Rick Woolard. Unknown to me, two guys on the Blue Team went to Woolard and complained.

Both were younger, hard-charging—at least physically—and held some sway with their peers. They figured this was their unit and Woolard would side with them.

"Hey, this officer, he thinks he knows it all," they told him. "He's not listening to us. He's a problem."

That was why Woolard called me into his office. He was a Vietnam vet who came out of central casting for what a SEAL should be. Woolard had a lean swimmer's physique with rugged good looks and a confident demeanor that made him a natural leader in the SEAL community. He was destined to be an admiral in the not-too-distant future.

This wasn't an office call to see how I was doing. This was a corrective action.

"Hey, Bob, I'm hearing that you're a problem in the team," he said after I'd sat down in a stiff chair across from his desk. "You don't listen to them."

Confrontation is tough because the first reaction is usually defensive. What did he mean I didn't listen? I was the commander of the team. I couldn't break through their culture because they weren't open-minded. They knew it all, and because they were at Dam Neck, that bred entitlement. The experience in their minds was based on longevity at the team, as opposed to anything else. And that justified their ability to question leadership. They were myopic. They didn't have any knowledge outside of the experience they were in and their standards were predicated on that and that alone. There was no sharing the Gouge.

I took a deep breath before I spoke.

"Sir, that's not at all the case," I said, holding back anger. "We can't execute the mission. And they're not focused on that, sir."

I spent the next few minutes laying out the issues I saw in the team. Some of the guys drank too much. They weren't in shape. I told Woolard the team I left to join the command in Dam Neck was better.

"We're the national force," I said. "But we don't act like it."

Woolard listened with his arms crossed in front of his chest. When I finished, he leaned forward and rested his forearms on the desk.

"Your response confirmed what I am hearing," he said.

It was a gut punch. What the hell was he talking about? It was clear he was taking the team's side and hadn't listened to a word I said. He wasn't interested in what the new officer thought. He was stuck in the same echo chamber trapped behind the Dam Neck fence. I left believing my career at the command was over, which had been the case for many of my compatriots, including Bill McRaven, Frank Schooley, and other officers who were much better than I. The whole episode left me in a funk. I was sure Woolard was going to fire me the next morning.

On my ride home, I tried to make sense of what had happened. My career had always benefitted from the Gouge. My actions were directed by my desire to live up to my contract with my teammates. Being accountable for my actions and for my team. Thinking about the community over the individual. But instead of elevating all around me, I'd isolated myself and it likely cost me a job.

The next morning, I got the dreaded call to report to Woolard's office. I threw on a uniform and headed to the skipper's office. I was shocked by the skipper's demeanor. Instead of crossed arms, Woolard was relaxed. He seemed relieved.

"OK, Bob," Woolard said. "I think you know what you're doing. Go forth and continue fighting the battle."

I much preferred this option as opposed to being fired, but I was a little shocked. It was a 180-degree turn. After I left his office, I learned three weeks earlier, the command had been subjected to a unit-wide urine analysis test, a standard procedure in the Navy to deter drug use. The results came back that morning. Not by design. I was very lucky. One of the guys who talked to Woolard popped positive for cocaine.

Luck can be more relevant than competency sometimes and I had built a career on it. But had I not understood or could manage confrontational leadership, there was no way to correct the situation. Once the two guys were gone, things started coming around. Addition by subtraction. I think the other guys saw the consequences of ignoring good order and discipline. So that confrontation, that accountability, and the price reinforced how vulnerable the status quo culture had been.

Getting rid of some of the ring leaders, or at least instigators, changed the culture for a while. But I soon rotated out and some of it has slipped back in, especially after all the fanfare SEALs enjoyed since 2001. It's funny—Bill McRaven is famous for leading the SEALs during the Osama bin Laden mission, but he was fired from the team at Dam Neck before I arrived for exactly the same sort of situation I encountered. He challenged their operational expertise, their ethics, their military demeanor, and professionalism and he left the command because of it, willing to jeopardize his career, while maintaining his values. He will always be my hero and I respect him more for this than I do for the raid that killed Osama bin Laden.

Part of the Gouge is understanding when you need to confront something—how to ensure it is not adversarial, and how to positively leverage it to meet your objectives. Challenging each other is healthy. Because of it, the best ideas and best concepts will win the day. For the Gouge to work for the welfare of all, leaders must be willing to confront individuals and challenge them.

It takes a lot of faith in yourself to be able to confront these types of issues, especially in insular cultures like Special Operations. But confrontation is healthy. If you're not feeling it, you're not pushing hard enough to learn and better yourself and your organization. If someone doesn't stand up and challenge your concepts, challenge your ideas, and confront you on them, then you're not going to get the best out of yourself or your team.

I embrace that.

I try to encourage people to stand up and speak their minds. Open communication is one of the principles of the Gouge. And with that comes confrontation. It's healthy. It doesn't need to be adversarial, but it's the ability to challenge what's right, what's wrong, and what's experience-based or not. You need to have compelling, irrefutable logic and understand that at the end of the confrontation you both comprehend not only the problem but also that the thought process and solutions are just as important. If you do that in an open, transparent, and collaborative way, it's a process. It's accepted. Most importantly, you probably come up with the best solution.

Look at Elon Musk; look at so many of these guys who are changing society. I would tell you they're confrontational. They're going to buck the system. They're going to fight for what they think is right. And more importantly, they're going to articulate and express their logic.

Confrontation is easier to manage in the military because of the rigid chain of command. It is messier in the corporate sector because, from my experience, no one will ever confront anyone. No one will challenge. It's all about going along with the flow.

At my recent company, we had a program to provide a world-class command and control system as the backbone of one of the most capable militaries in the Middle East. Everyone supported the program, but it took seven years to deliver because the first guy in charge just wanted to sell the program, knowing it was a program we would not and could not execute. I pushed back in meetings and emails.

"Hey, guys, we can't execute."

Each time I was told we were going to be fine. But we kept going around the problem until our customer—a foreign senior military official—blasted us in a meeting.

"This is the worst program we've ever had," he told the woman in charge of executing it. "We're going to cancel and get rid of it."

We came out of the meeting and everyone was shell-shocked. I was the only one smiling.

"This is the worst meeting I've ever been in in my life," the executive said.

I shook my head. "That's the best meeting we've ever had on this program."

The executive thought I was joking. I wasn't. The military official told us exactly what we needed to do to fix it.

"What you've got to do is put someone out here to run the program," I said.

After that meeting, we sent someone overseas to run the program and we turned the program around. That executive lasted for a few months and then rotated to another job. Another guy took over and started running it from the United States again. The program was approaching IOC—initial operating capability—and we needed to meet the requirements of the program to get paid. We weren't meeting that mark, so the customer wasn't going to pay us. The new executive was reporting that the program was running smoothly. But I told my boss things weren't going well. My boss told me to write a letter to the head of the company, telling him regardless of what everyone tells you, this program is in big trouble. The guy running the program called me when he learned of the letter.

"You threw me under the bus," he said.

"Yeah, I threw you under the bus," I said. "I told you I would. Because the program is failing, and we are not going to get paid. You must get out here and work it with the customer. You can't run this from the United States."

"Bob, I've got to get paid or I'm going to lose this," he said.

The confrontation ended with us coming up with a plan. I went in with him to sell the customer on an extension so we could meet the IOC requirements. I had to challenge him and fight him every step of the way, but we finally got it all done and delivered three years late, and the whole program took us seven years when it should have been done in four.

We had to challenge the company to do the right thing for the customer. We need to do the same now in our country. We cannot stand divided. We cannot let unhealthy confrontation dominate. Now, I'm not saying don't stand up for your ideals, but do it with an ear toward understanding and acceptance, maybe even compromise. Confrontation only works when it is treated as a means to meet everyone's objectives, not to win a fight. It is a means to take on obstacles for progress. It is a powerful and constructive tool if used properly. During confrontation, don't abandon the rest of the Gouge. We're still one community with a purpose. Our contract with one another is not void when we don't agree. Scorched-earth confrontation only creates a place no one wants to live. Use other methods when you can, but accept confrontation as a part of life.

That's the Gouge. Come prepared.

Physical Training (PT) with friends, teammates, is a powerful and rewarding experience. The bonding experience pays dividends in every way. It should be a daily event for all.

CHAPTER 14

Change and Transition Are Inevitable

It's not the change that makes it hard for service members to take off the uniform—hell, we're used to deploying and changing jobs frequently—it's the change in purpose.

Purpose is the engine that drives you. It's the thing that makes you put two feet on the floor in the morning and get to work. You come into the military with a defined purpose. In fact, that's what attracts most people to the service. The message that you're going to serve your country. You're going to do what your country needs. But in many ways, a transition into civilian life—the pivot—may be as much of an achievement as a long military career.

Many military men and women commonly face pitfalls in their transitions to civilian life by applying the same philosophy that helped them make critical decisions in combat and rise in the ranks. I used the Gouge. It proved a way of seeing the world that also helped me smoothly transition to civilian life and thrive in a completely new work environment.

But others struggle.

One indicator of this struggle is the suicide rates among our veterans. I believe suicide can be a byproduct of a service member taking off their uniform and losing their purpose. That is why transition is always so difficult and uncertain. We've been at war for the last twenty years, which has only served to reinforce our purpose and validated everything we came into the military to do and sacrificed for. It's tough to replace that purpose in the civilian world. Nothing means as much, nor has the impact.

For our enlisted members, it's even more of a challenge than the officer corps. Take my SEAL son-in-law. All that he's done for the last decade and a half is deploy and be a shooter and operator. He lives for it. He wants to be a perfectionist and be the best SEAL possible. What happens when he leaves the Navy? Can he find that same sort of purpose, that validation, if he's doing the budget for a project or working on a contract?

That's going to be tough after spending his days in combat with some of America's best warriors. I think officers have a better go of it because of their career path. Officers change jobs every two years and many jobs can be completely different than the one we had before. We're trained to reinvent ourselves and adjust to new environments. Military members understand the need to apply themselves and accomplish a completely different objective in a different environment.

We start by validating our first six to eight years in the Navy at the tactical level.

You're an aviator. You're a SEAL. You're a submariner. You become proficient in the skills associated with that warfare specialty. But officers quickly transition to the operational level as an operations officer and then the executive officer. If you're successful there, you head to the strategic level. Each time you get further from being a "shooter." Your purpose changes throughout your career, which is a much different dynamic than our enlisted ranks.

And I don't know if we prepare them—educate them—for the transition.

We know how to make the best SEALs or special forces soldiers, but we don't open up the aperture and show them what they can do with their skills and how it translates in the civilian world.

We fail to balance professional training with the same kind of personal training. And that's some of why the Gouge is so important. We're focusing on that personal attention. Those are tools and processes that help you balance that professional training with those personal skills you need to take care of your family, to take care of yourself, to understand what you're going to do with your money so that when you do leave the service, you're in a position where you have choices. You're not forced into something that you don't enjoy and that lacks the same purpose.

When I retired after almost forty years in the Navy, I counted up all my jobs and landed on twenty-six. I transitioned twenty-six different times and each time I had to adapt to a new purpose. I also never got used to the trappings of being a senior officer. My nickname around the teams was "Big Bob." I liked being with the guys. I never drank my own Kool-Aid. I stayed grounded. Yeah, I was *Admiral Harward*, but more specifically I never forgot I was just Bob Harward.

When I came out of both Afghanistan and Iraq, I went to the White House and became a member of a team. It wasn't my show and presidential power will humble even the proudest man. They saw me as another member of the team who could bring expertise from my military background to help shape what we did politically and economically to shape policy.

The same thing happened when I took over Middle East operations as a defense contractor. When I transitioned, I took the uniform off, but it was the same sort of thing. I was falling in on a team with a purpose to help foster relations with our allies in the Middle East region and help build their national security capabilities. I understood the culture. I understood the people. I understood our role in supporting national security by helping our partners build capabilities with products we have. I was very fortunate in that transition because a lot of those things I had done in a variety of military jobs applied and I could leverage my experience.

Bring what you can to the table and contribute, and others will help you succeed.

I went from driving ships to a SEAL. That was completely different. I went from the SEAL team to Dam Neck, which was completely different. Then I went to a regular Navy staff with the Marines in Japan. That was different. Then I was in the Philippines as the executive officer and then the Naval War College. This trend of new and different jobs never ended (working at the White House, invading countries, running prisons). Every job was completely different, and I knew very little about it going in, but because of the people I worked with and the way we worked collectively using the Gouge, we all succeeded.

But even for me, success was predicated on finding that purpose. If you can't find that purpose, then that may not be the best gig for you. But don't belittle the purpose of taking care of your family. Taking care of your family is as noble and powerful as any other purpose. If you can't believe in the purpose, be it contributing to a company or taking care of your family with the funds you're earning, that's going to be a problem.

So is the challenge of asking for help. You've got to leverage your network for mentors and for people who can help you. That's what the Gouge does. It builds networks and paths to build rapport with anyone and everyone. It's people who you have trust and confidence in who are in that same place seven or eight years before. Identifying that network is key. Don't be afraid to ask. Be proactive in going out and sharing the Gouge. I spend half my time talking to people about jobs, opportunities, what they can do, and what we can do. Building those networks, leveraging those networks, and supporting those networks are important.

All transitions are difficult but also exciting. There's risk. There's fear. There isn't one job that I thought I could do or I knew. I was always concerned about, *oh boy, they're going to find out this is beyond me*, but you always work through that and before long, just like you're in the military, you become a great asset.

CHAPTER 15

As a Human Race, We Are Doing Pretty Damn Good

I've currently lived in the Middle East for nearly a decade. For me, it was a homecoming. I'd essentially grown up in Iran, so this part of the world—the smell of the souk, the echo of the call to prayer at dawn, and the culture of close-knit families and leaving everything in the hands of Allah—was familiar. I'd dare say more comfortable than the hustle of America, the country I spent most of my life serving.

But it never fails that people ask me how I can live in the Middle East.

Isn't it dangerous? Aren't you afraid?

They obviously have no idea. The United Arab Emirates is one of the safest countries on the planet. I would feel perfectly safe sleeping outside in a park at night in many places in this region, as many do. The people are warm, loving, and family oriented. The leadership is humble, gracious, and progressive. People around the world flock to live here, as I have.

I think the issue is that, in general, people have a fear of others and things they do not understand. I consider myself lucky to have spent seven years of my childhood growing up in the Middle East because I learned first-hand how kind and generous these people are. It is an essential element of their culture.

When I led our troops into Afghanistan, I came across an instance when this very Gouge saved my life and those around me. I was traveling with a group of our guys through Lashkar Ghar the first week of October 2001 and many of the alleys were blocked. At one point, we hit another blocked alley and came face-to-face with fifteen men pointing guns at us. The men in my vehicle immediately raised their weapons. There we all were, staring at each other with all of our weapons drawn. It was a stand-off. I had to decide how we were going to proceed. I got out of my vehicle and walked toward the barricades.

"Move out of the way," I said to the Afghan men in Farsi. "Move. We are going through."

I started to move the barricades myself. I can't say that I wasn't relieved when the Afghan men stepped aside and let us pass, unharmed.

Speaking their language didn't hurt. Today, almost everyone speaks some level of English. Language can still be a barrier, but not like it was years ago. When I was a child living in the Middle East, I came to realize that understanding a different language was like opening the window to a new culture. I could understand the humor and the grief. The idiosyncrasies of any culture can be understood in its language and I feel fortunate that I had the opportunity to explore a different language and culture as a child. It's likely that my speaking Farsi also helped in this situation. I was perhaps less foreign to these Afghani men holding guns because of it. The language allowed me to traverse between the two groups, the two cultures, safely.

But more than the language, it was that Gouge, that belief, that most people are not trying to hurt you, that saved not only my life, but a whole bunch of lives that day. Had I ordered my men to shoot, or had they opened fire independently simply because there were guns pointing at us, those other men surely would have fired back. We would have lost men on our side. They would have lost men on their side. Many injuries would have been incurred. An experience like that would have stayed with everyone for the rest of their lives and would have harmed our soldiers' relationships with the Afghan people, who I knew as kind and generous.

This same situation played out in Iraq when we were confronted by a half dozen Iranian gunboats that surrounded us and threatened to kill us if we went up the Shatt al-Arab (River of the Arabs).

After we seized the oil platforms, we were transitioning to the battle for Basra. Our mission was to control the waterways coming in and out of the Iraqi port. We boarded four Special Operations armored riverine patrol boats from our afloat staging base. We were going to go up the Shatt al-Arab, which divides Iran and Iraq.

The river is formed by the confluence of the Euphrates and the Tigris rivers and both countries have been at odds over its navigation rights. The eight-year Iran-Iraq War was sparked in part over control of the river. For us, the Shatt al-Arab was important because it was Iraq's outlet to the Arabian Gulf. We needed it to ship humanitarian aid into Iraq and get oil out.

My flotilla of riverine boats launched from a high-speed vessel (HSV) in the Arabian Gulf and headed north for the mouth of the river. In addition to the American crews, we had Kuwaiti commandos on board as well. To show our intent, we put American and Iranian flags on the side to show we came in peace and respected the Iranians. We were about five miles from the coast when a half dozen Iranian small boats—similar to Boston Whalers—intercepted us. The Iranian crews were dressed in camouflage uniforms and had AK-47 rifles and RPGs. The Iranian boats were about thirty yards off our starboard side. I raised a bullhorn and in Farsi, told them our intention to cruise up the Shatt al-Arab.

They didn't respond. Instead, they closed on our boats. At close range, their RPGs were useless and our machine guns—.50 caliber heavy machine guns, M60 light machine guns, and 40mm automatic grenade launchers—had them outgunned. If they fired, it would be a short fight and we'd end up on the better end of it.

I knew it. They knew it. I was confident no one was shooting anyone.

I ordered my flotilla to continue toward the mouth of the river. My guys on the Al-Faw peninsula already took some ineffective fire from the Iranian side of the river. It wasn't an attack. More like a show of force. This was the same thing. I was determined to keep the rounds in the guns this time.

"Hey, sir, just so you know, there are a bunch of Iranian boats starting to block the mouth," was the radio report we received from our guys on the peninsula who could observe the mouth of the Shatt al-Arab. They video linked pictures they were taking showing more Iranian boats blockading the mouth of the Shatt al-Arab.

"OK," I said. "Keep going. That won't be an issue. I think they'll take off when we get up there."

As we got closer, a sixty-five-foot Iranian Boghammar crossed our bow and demonstrated hostile intent. It had a DShK machine gun on it, but it was still under-gunned compared to my patrol boats. But unlike the smaller boats, the DShK crew turned its gun to face our lead boat. My crews responded in kind, turning our heavy machine guns toward the patrol boat. The captain of the Iranian boat called on radio and was yelling over a bullhorn.

"Halt," he said. "If you continue toward the Shatt, we will open fire."

It was an empty threat. We could take them out, but before I started a war with Iran, I called up to my higher headquarters. I ordered my boats to cut their engines and hold any fire, as we were surrounded by this group of Iranian boats who clearly did not want us entering the Shatt al-Arab. We shot pictures of the Iranian boats and sent them to the Fifth Fleet Commander, Admiral Willie Moore. I then got on the radio with him.

"Just so you know, they're blocking us; they're pointing guns at us; they tell us they're going to kill us," I said over the radio to the admiral in charge of naval forces in the Arabian Gulf. "This is international waters. I have freedom of navigation. I wanted to let you know before I engaged all these Iranians."

I knew the headquarters was freaking out on the other end of the radio. That kind of made me smile. The Iranians continued to circle us while we waited. No one shot. It was a standoff. I passed word to my crew not to shoot unless engaged. The headquarters finally came back with guidance. We weren't at war with Iran. Find another way to the Shatt al-Arab.

"That's bullshit," I called back. "We have the right of freedom of navigation, and they are clearly demonstrating hostile intent. They're threatening us. I believe we should demonstrate force here and kill all these guys as a message to Iran not to try to expand their power. We're cleared by the Iraqis. We're going up their side of the waterway. We should not allow Iran to stop that."

Headquarters' response came right away. "Negative. Find another way to get to Basra."

I don't run into brick walls. Once I'm told no and after I reinforce my position and I'm told no again, I follow orders. Luckily, I had a hunch this might happen. I made the call and soon we heard the thump of helicopter engines. Over the horizon I saw three CH-46 Sea Knight helicopters. The aircraft resembles Army Chinooks with two massive rotors—one in the front and one in the back. The helicopters flew over us and then circled around and dropped cables. The crews attached the cables to strongpoints on the boats and within minutes of their arrival we were airborne. I looked over the side of the boat so I could see the astonished faces of the Iranians on the patrol boat as we waved goodbye.

Once we were clear, the helicopters put all three boats into the water on the Iraqi side of the river and we continued our patrol to Basra. It was such an elegant use of capabilities to meet the mission and avoid death and conflict when we didn't have to because our policy at the time was not to engage the Iranians. We took the moral high ground to avoid conflict and meet our broader objectives of going into Iraq.

In most cases, we found we didn't need to shoot. We avoided conflict, even though it may have been called for.

Everyone's got guns. It didn't mean they were trained or knew how to use them, or wanted to get in a fight with our overwhelming firepower. I accepted that risk and I ran into that scenario more times than not in Afghanistan and Iraq. This is what I mean when I say that the benefits of the Gouge grow and build over time. That lesson learned while hitchhiking as a child helped to spare a handful of lives and protect international relations decades later.

Both sides were fearful. Apprehensive. No well-adjusted human takes a life without paying a price. Fear is a part of life. It is a guide. Sometimes it tells us what not to do. Sometimes it keeps us focused, like when you're trying to land on top of Mount Everest in a parachute. It is an emotion we've all felt and understand.

Good Gouge helps alleviate that fear.

It's been a tough couple of years in the world, so it is easy for fear to take over. We've experienced a global pandemic, economic upheaval, and the protest on the US Capitol on January 6, 2021.

If you're like many people these days, you probably believe that the world is pretty screwed up. Crazy stuff is happening all the time, around every corner. Right? Well, I don't buy into that narrative because crazy things have been happening since the beginning of time. There has always been some boogeyman whom we have had to guard ourselves against.

Here is the Gouge.

What has changed, in more recent times, is the context. The fear that is pushed on us and that many people carry around with them is completely distorted and out of proportion to the threat itself. Let me tell you, we are not facing near-term existential threats. The world is not coming to an end. The sky is not falling. Yes, shit happens—all the time. But it doesn't mean that we need to change the way we live. It doesn't mean that this fear needs to confine us and take away the adventure that is life.

Look at the world right now.

We have nearly eradicated starvation. Disease, yeah, we're in a global pandemic that will likely be with us forever, but if you remember, we had polio, we had yellow fever, we had cholera—we had so many illnesses and diseases that have been eradicated because of vaccinations. Medically, cancer is still the big bugaboo, but when I can walk into a hospital, have heart surgery, and walk out three or four hours later without even cracking my chest, medicine has made incredible leaps and bounds. Our average life span is beyond anything anyone ever expected.

The world is safer and more connected than it ever has been in history. Thanks to the internet and cellular technology, every individual in the world has access to more information and more opportunities. Mankind in general is doing much better than we've ever done before.

That doesn't mean we're devoid of problems.

Racism and bias are still within our systems worldwide and we need to be deliberate about rooting it out. We need to bend our arc toward justice and equity. And we have to address our climate crisis. The Department of Defense has led the way on much of this because we understand it is a national security crisis.

But don't lose focus on the whole picture by only looking at what isn't working. In general, we're on the right track, folks. And the opportunities and technology are only enhancing that and improving that at a rate we've never seen before.

The reality is that a big industry has sprung up since September 11, 2001—the security industry. Many people's careers have been bolstered as a result of this fear. Many people have made a lot of money on this fear. It's almost taken on a life of its own. But again, in my opinion, it is greatly exaggerated to the threats we actually face. To put everything in context, we each have a one in over 4,500,000 chance of being killed by foreign-born terrorists. You're more likely to die from a heat wave or animal attack, or, sadly, suicide. Now, let me be clear. We needed to establish security and safety protocols after the attacks on the World Trade Center and the Pentagon. We still need to maintain safety protocols. We need to be safe. But billions of dollars' worth of safety protocols? An army of security personnel who are trained to blindly adhere to procedures at the cost of rational thinking or common sense. I'm not so sure about that.

We have a submarine base by my house and I sometimes go there to use the gym. Now, as you enter, you go through a gate manned by a guard. Then, a hundred yards down, there's a guard shack with some guy who sits there all day, waiting for someone to run the gate—which, by the way, is probably never going to happen. Now, should this happen, he can throw up the tire puncture barrier in an attempt to stop the car. But, really, even if someone was going to run the gate, they have no way of accessing anything else of importance as all the valuable assets are isolated by another set of guards and infrastructure. So, this poor guard's job in life is to sit in this shack all day and wait for the "possible event" to happen, which I would wager will never happen.

This is a great example of wasting manpower.

I have witnessed for over eight years equating to many years of manpower—a career of sitting in a shack waiting for something bad to happen in addition to a whole bunch of money and hours on a fear that has been completely distorted. It's a way to add another layer of security to something that's somewhat improbable, if not irrelevant. I imagine this is happening around the world.

Another case in point: When I was in Afghanistan on my last tour, I ran a prison in the middle of nowhere. At some point, someone felt that there was a big enough threat of a mortar attack that they built these huge block walls, barriers of sorts, around the entire complex that no one could shoot through, protect from blasts, or get past. Millions of dollars went into these barriers. Fine. But then that wasn't enough. There was still fear. So, some folks decided that they needed to also wall off the other side of the road of the first barrier wall. Realistically, no one cared about the few lone people driving in their cars to the prison. They cared about getting to the prison. But we spent millions of dollars on this security project in total, and, in my estimation, it didn't really make anyone any more secure. But it sure as hell made some folks a lot of money. The actions taken were so out of context to the situation itself. The Gouge here is to understand your fear. In these instances, the fear that drove these additional security measures was more harmful than the risks themselves.

Just because I'm on a roll with this topic, I'll give you one more example. I had just taken over as deputy commander at US Central Command when I arrived in Washington, DC, on my first official business trip in my new post. I got to the hotel and there was a four-person security detail there waiting for me.

Me! A Navy SEAL traveling in the United States.

"Who did this?" I asked.

Evidently, the former commander had set up the detail for himself and so I inherited it. Now, I can't really speak for him. Maybe he felt that he couldn't protect himself, but this is the United States and I can think of very few military leaders that need protection in our own country. I quickly got rid of that detail. The threat did not justify the manpower and cost.

Many of these security details have become more of a status symbol than a security operation. We spend millions of dollars on groups of bodyguards for anyone who thinks they are important. But they aren't all necessary. Again, the risk is not aligned to the cost and the security industry continues to balloon. The industry itself seems to do more to sustain itself than to fulfill any realistic threat or operational requirement. A self-licking ice cream cone. We have come to live our lives and spend valuable resources based on what might happen rather than on what is likely to happen.

The Gouge here: don't buy into the hype and base your fear on reality.

Outside of the government and military, this same bloated fear has bled into all areas of our culture. The reality is that fear taken out of context is detrimental to everyone. It impacts families, children, and businesses. You can't let bum Gouge scare you off your path. I have a friend, for example, who thinks it's so cool that I hitchhiked all over as a teenager, so I suggested that he give his son the same opportunity.

"Oh no," he told me. "I would be too nervous that something would happen to him."

Maybe something would happen. And maybe it wouldn't. This father is buying into the fear rather than the reward, which, in my opinion, is so much greater. When you let fear make your decisions, you relinquish your belief in yourself or in another person.

And that robs everyone of a whole lot of important life experience.

CHAPTER 16

Good Gouge

The Gouge and the philosophy my father taught me, and how applicable it was to everything I did, played out throughout my life in ways I never would have imagined.

I've lived by it since my youth. My father taught me the philosophy through his words and actions. He showed me the power of taking care of people first, and like Maslow's hierarchy—shelter, food, etc.—if you take care of the team, the team will take care of the mission. It is a proactive and incessant focus on people and helping them accomplish a mission.

I've done this religiously my whole career because my dad, and other leaders I followed, did the same. The Gouge he passed to me went from the very mundane and tactical to the most strategic, and always with lifelong ramifications. As an example, I offer some unique pieces of Gouge that are applicable to most of my family in uniform and they served as starting blocks for how I inculcated the Gouge in others. It is also the Gouge that I've shared with most of my teammates and others, but it is also the hardest for people to assimilate as it sounds weird and makes me seem like a salesman. In reality it has paid off so well for me that I want everyone I care for to know about it. Hopefully they would do the same with others they served and worked with.

The most pertinent Gouge (to my career) that my dad gave me as I started my naval career had to do with the annual performance reviews that everyone in the Navy receives. These reviews are known as Fitness Reports (FITREPs) and are especially important if you plan to remain in the military and move up in your career. Whatever is written in this report will eventually be reviewed by a random group of Naval Officers who may not personally know the boss who wrote the report or the person whose report they are reviewing. The result of this review determines whether this individual officer will be promoted and thereby allowed to stay in uniform and serve or leave the service. Bottom line: FITREPs are important.

My dad explained to me the importance of the FITREPs, but also that they are a pain in the ass for every boss who must write them.

"People are busy," he explained. "You want to find a way to make your bosses' lives easier."

His idea was for me to get the right forms from the admin office at the right time, figure out what the report needed to say, and write it all myself. I was to hand in the report to my boss a week before it was due. My dad's logic was that if I was doing a good job and my boss liked me, they would probably just sign it. If not, they would call me in to discuss what they disagree with, which would be invaluable information and feedback for me. Either way, I made the process easier, which would separate me from my colleagues who would be vying for the same promotions and get feedback on my performance. In my thirty-four years of FITREPs, there was only one occasion where my boss did not immediately sign my submitted performance review, with the caveat being on a few occasions they added words or mentored me on how to make it stronger to be more effective at the promotion boards as well as what would be needed for future promotions.

I find it ironic that my father always told me I would be an admiral one day, but I never thought I was going to be good enough. His Gouge about the FITREPs ended up serving as the critical enabler allowing me to progress up through the ranks to ultimately be selected for admiral. The heart of my father's Gouge in this instance was how to separate yourself from your pack and always for the right reasons.

When I graduated from the Naval Academy, I thought my father was going to give me a car or at least some money as a graduation present, as my logic concluded that I had saved him from shelling out for four years of college. Instead, he gave me two things:

A membership to the Army Navy Country Club in Arlington, Virginia, and a life insurance policy. At the time I was not impressed and did not see the value in these gifts.

Here's why this is good Gouge. At the time, if you graduated from any of the service academies as a newly commissioned officer, a lifetime membership to join the Army Navy Country Club was $100. If you buy it any other time it's going to cost significantly more. I didn't play golf when I graduated so I thought, *what the hell do I need this thing for?* Well, now I play golf and a membership would now cost me tens of thousands of dollars.

His second present was much more important and significant. A policy with Navy Mutual Aid Association (NMAA), which is basically one of two non-profit insurance companies (with the other being the Army and Airforce Mutual Aid Association). The two are almost in baseball throwing distance from each other in Northern Virginia, just across the Potomac from the Nation's Capital. When he gave me the policy, my first thought was, *what the hell do I need life insurance for?* and more importantly, it required me to make payments of seventy dollars a month. I was not a happy camper taking on this debt as I started my new career. The cash value had about one thousand dollars in it, so my intent was to cash it out. My dad could sense this and made me agree to make the payments for three more years. When he first purchased the policy, it required payments for seven years to be fully paid off, and he had made all the payments for the first four years, and now was adamant that I meet the obligation for the last three since I was gainfully employed. If at that point after being fully paid off, I did not think it was a good investment, then he would agree to me canceling the account and recovering the money. Needless to say, when I paid off the policy, I had come to realize the significant value of the reinvested tax-free benefits, and not only did I not cancel it, but I also bought all the insurance they would sell me. This was great Gouge, as it has only become more valuable to me and my family every year, providing financial security in so many ways.

These associations (Navy Mutual Aid Association and Army and Airforce Mutual Aid Association) were created when Americans conquered the West. In the late 1800s, if anyone in the military got killed, they would pass the hat for money to send the families back east, where everyone came from. Then Little

Bighorn happened and there was no one left to pass the hat. All the families were stuck out west with no way to get home. A bunch of military members went to Congress and asked to set up an association to take care of the families. As I understand it, this is how these two mutual aid associations were born.

All the money the members pay for in premiums is invested. The premiums and the return on the investments serve to pay for the small staff that runs it and to pay off death claims every year. The remaining annual revenue is then distributed to the members as dividends on an annual basis. It's basically free insurance as it guarantees that your cash value will always be equal to or greater than the amount you have paid into it. Just as important it has returned tax-free dividends that are reinvested each year, with the dividends always being much more significant than I would receive from any bank interest-drawing vehicle such as a CD. My premiums over the years, and subsequent returns, have resulted in a cash balance of over a million dollars while my death benefits have grown to many times that, providing all the insurance my family will ever need, all of which has been paid for.

What I once considered a lousy gift from my father has grown into real, hard cash and security for my family. The other benefits are just as powerful, providing a lifetime of benefits. As an example, most military members keep their important documents (wills, power of attorney, birth certificates, insurance policies, etc.) in a metal lock box at home, where they have access, and they take this with them wherever they move. Navy Mutual holds all of those for me for free.

When the wife and daughters were evacuated from the Philippines and went home to Tennessee, she needed their birth certificates to register for school. If they had still been with me in the Philippines, we would have had a problem. NMAA sent the school the certified copies in overnight mail, free of charge.

Bottom line: I have carefree and secure access to all my essential documents. Additionally, should I need any long-term medical care and any related housing needs, my NMAA policy will cover it from the death benefits. There is a plethora of other incredible benefits that come from being a member of this organization.

Finally, my father opened an account for me in the Navy Federal Credit Union, which has now become the largest credit union in the world. It has provided me with a lifetime of free banking, with the ability to do the bulk of my financial needs online from anywhere in the world at any time, unprecedented service, and the best possible rates on loans and savings. I always got my car and house insurance from USAA, and I covered all the services me and my family needed for the lowest costs possible. Important aspects to consider if you are pursuing a career in the military.

These are just a few examples of the wide range of Gouge I pass on to all of those I serve with. As a leader I believe it is just as important to share the personal experiences and benefits as it is the professional experiences that will help all my shipmates live a richer life. That in itself is good Gouge.

That's what leaders are supposed to do: share their knowledge, experience, and wisdom. It is up to the recipients to use it as they see fit.

EPILOGUE

The leather-bound book was thin with gold embossed letters. It was the 1972 Officers' Writing Guide, obviously oriented to a military professional.

My aide, a West Point graduate and Apache helicopter pilot who had flown combat missions in Iraq, Tiffany Glowaki, walked it into my office and threw it on my desk. It was March 21, 2013, and I was the deputy commander of CENTCOM.

"Hey, sir," Glowaki said. "Some guy just dropped off your book."

I looked up from my computer.

"What do you mean, my 'book'?"

The aide shrugged. "Well, some guy just dropped off this book," the aide said, sliding it onto my desk. "He said it's your book. He found it in Bahrain."

I looked at the book and didn't recognize it.

"Who was he?"

The aide didn't know.

"Well, go grab him."

The aide left to find him, leaving the book in my hands. I opened the cover and saw a message scrolled on the front page:

"To Bob Harward. Happy Nowruz 1973. Jabo Jablonski."

I looked at my desk calendar. It was March 21, 2013. I looked back at the inscription. Nowruz—Iranian New Year, also known as the Persian New Year—was on March 21. This message was written forty years ago to the day. But it wasn't written to me. It was written to my father. I'm Bob Harward, Jr.

Harvey "Jabo" Jablonski was a West Point football god. He was one of their star players and served as captain of the team in 1933. Army went 9-1 that year and outscored its opponents 227 to 26. He later went on to coach the team. He served in three wars—World War II and the Korean and Vietnam wars. His last tour coming out of Vietnam was as the head military advisor in Iran. My father was his Navy component commander in 1968 and they both would transition after retiring from the military into the defense industry in Iran in the 1970s, where Jabo was with Northrop Grumman, and my dad with Ingalls Shipbuilding and Harris Radio. They were drinking buddies, and it is a tradition on Nowruz to give gifts, often books. Whoever found this book looked at it and figured *Bob Harward* was Admiral Harward. If I hadn't been a well-known admiral, this book would've never gotten to me.

The hair went up on the back of my neck because my father told me after I graduated from the Naval Academy that I'd end up being an admiral one day. I never dreamed it was possible.

After spending four years on a ship and serving as a surface warfare officer, as my father did for thirty-two years, I was focused on becoming a Navy SEAL. When I transferred to the SEALs, he was aghast.

"Dammit, I never did think you were too bright; I just didn't think you were this dumb," he told me. "There's no future in that SEALs shit."

"To hell with that, Dad. I think I'm better at this, and this is what I want to do."

It was the one time I did not go with my father's advice. I knew what was better for me and for years he really had his doubts until he finally admitted I made a good call after coincidently becoming drinking buddies with Dick Marcinko, my former commander and the founder of SEAL Team SIX. After leaving Iran after the collapse of the Shah in 1979, my father ended up in DC, continuing to work in the US defense industry. Dick was sequestered in DC after being relieved from SEAL Team SIX while being investigated, for which he was later indicted. They both happened to find the basement bar at the Fort Myer Officers' Club, their sort of haunt and obviously had a lot in common (including me and drinking) after bumping into each other. From that point on, my father was always insistent that I would be an admiral one day.

"Dad, we only have a few captains and no admirals in the SEAL community," I said. "I'll be lucky if I make captain and do a twenty-year career."

My dad just shook his head and patted me on the shoulder. "Nah, I can see it in you. You're going to be an admiral."

He had so much faith in me. I was living the life he loved, and he kept insisting that I would be an admiral. One of my greatest regrets (and not that I could control it) is that he passed away before I pinned on the stars.

To this day, we never figured out who delivered the book. But in my heart, I know it was my father. I know my father was in heaven looking at me, and this "visiting trip" was his means of letting me know he was right. The book reaffirmed my faith in the things I could not see and was proof to me there is more to life than anything on this planet. I don't know if it's under Allah's rules, God's rules, or anyone's rules. I do know my father sent the book to me as a message.

"Hey, dumbass, I'm still watching, and I told you you'd make admiral one day."

Damn, he was right!

This incident served as an affirmation of everything that had happened in my life and directly related to the Gouge in what it did for me and how much, and why, my father had inculcated it into my thinking. In addition to my father's wisdom, I was blessed to work with people like General Wayne Downing, General Jim Mattis, President George Bush, and others who all set the standard for how to treat people and demonstrate the philosophy of the Gouge. Sharing and taking care of people and your contract with humanity will pay you back in ways you can't imagine possible.

The Gouge was my North Star. It guided me in my interactions with people, which resulted in so many great experiences and adventures in life, enhancing all of it. While enabling and determining my life in so many ways, I hope and believe the Gouge had the same impact on other people's lives. I also contribute the Gouge to my proudest professional accomplishment—never losing a single man or woman under my command. Every service person that I deployed, put into combat, decades' worth of day-in-and-day-out hazard training that I conducted and was responsible for, came home and without injury. In some respects, I consider this a miracle, but I also know that it was the result of detailed planning and understanding of how to mitigate risk and the collective wisdom and experience of so many over so many years. All of these are testaments to the Gouge.

The Gouge's application can stretch so much further. Its benefits can reach sports teams, businesses, families, and beyond. The Gouge can be applied to leadership, entrepreneurship, team building, family issues, education, physical and emotional well-being, you name it. The Gouge is designed to make you better, smarter, and prepared for any situation. It is general in context, though the beauty of this philosophy is that it can be translated to apply to any area of anyone's life.

Identify your own Gouge. Think about the essential personal and professional information you want your employees, team, and children to know. Focus on empowering those around you instead of yourself and watch how successful you become. Put yourself on a metaphorical bridge wing while underway and be accountable to your crew. Always look to better yourself and better those around you, and always be courageous enough to communicate it.

From my first command as a ship driver to my last assignment as deputy commander of all American forces in the Middle East, I'd brought the Gouge philosophy. It was the connective tissue to my leadership style. It was the lens through which I saw the world—a better, optimistic world. That hasn't changed. I was fortunate to live my purpose. That is success for me.

Since I've left the Navy, people often thank me and other veterans for our service. For me, it's almost embarrassing when it happens. I know it is well-meaning, but I do not think they realize I had the greatest adventure known to man. It should be me thanking them for paying taxes. I couldn't wait to wake up and see what adventure I faced that day. I felt the same way in my career in corporate America. Living your purpose makes life easier.

But I'm retiring—again, and for the third time, some time in the not-too-distant future from the defense and high-tech industry. I have had a decade of business in the defense industry outside the uniform. It has given me and my family a level of financial security we did not have when we left the Navy.

But it is time for a new adventure. A new purpose. This book is that next adventure.

My purpose with the time left in this world is to help others make the Gouge part of their lives. But the Gouge is personal. This book spells out how I used it—to great success—and it might not be exactly how you use it. But that is what makes it powerful.

The Gouge is very simple. It is information used to create a better outcome for all. It is a mindset that starts with finding that one thing that gets you excited and using that as fuel to help others find that spark. It is owning your actions and keeping others accountable for their actions. It is about banding together and taking on the bigger world, be it a massive ocean or that tricky relationship with a co-worker.

Life sometimes feels insurmountable and isolating. It is all about perspective. At the end of the day, the Gouge helps manage life and in doing so creates a better world. Share your purpose. Look out for one another. Most of all, always work toward better, be it in life, a community, or the world. My method on how to use the Gouge to do that is in these pages.

Go find yours.

ACKNOWLEDGMENTS

Without my swim buddies for the last decade,

Adam Nathanson
Mike Hanlin

this book would have never happened. They understand The Gouge! better than me.

Special thanks: Jeannine Imperiale, Stephanie Freid-Perenchio, Mo Gannon, Philomena Perera, Frank Weimann, Kevin Maurer, Alex Novak, Caitlin Burdette, and the entire team at Post Hill.

ABOUT THE AUTHOR

Robert (Bob) Harward was born in Newport, Rhode Island, to a US Navy family and spent his formative years in Iran, where he graduated from the Tehran American School. His father was a Navy captain and advised the Iranian Navy from 1968 to 1979. At the behest of his father, Bob enlisted in the Navy to attend the Naval Academy Prep School. He continued his education at the United States Naval Academy in Annapolis, Maryland, graduating in 1979 after earning a Bachelor of Science. He subsequently attended the Naval War College for his master's in International Security and Strategy. Harward began his military career as a Surface Warfare officer, navigating ships around the world, and then transferred to the Naval Special Warfare community, serving as a Navy SEAL for over thirty-two years. He held various leadership positions throughout his forty-year naval career, commanding a plethora of combat units in Bosnia, Afghanistan, Iraq, Kuwait, and Yemen, as well as a Nation Building Task Force in Afghanistan where he was responsible for building Rule of Law. He is currently the Executive Vice President for International Business and Strategy of Shield AI, where he is responsible for growing the company's international business operations and strategy on every continent. Before joining Shield AI, he was the Chief Executive of Lockheed Martin's International Business for eight years in the Middle East. He has been recognized as one of *Forbes'* Most Influential CEOs in the Middle East, and President Trump asked him to serve as his National Security Advisor.

Printed in Great Britain
by Amazon

49460738R00099